FREE TO BE *Fabulous*

"Resilient through personal heartache and tragedy, Debbie pressed into the Lord where she found peace and grace. More than appearance, beauty stems from being all that God created you to be. No matter your age, you can experience beauty and honor, and Debbie shows you how."

—**PeggySue Wells**, *Wall Street Journal* and *USA Today* bestselling author of *The Slave Across the Street, Rediscovering Your Happily Ever After,* and *Für Elise*

"Debbie Hardy is the kind of lady we all want to have as our next door neighbor or best friend. She exudes warmth, confidence, and humor. *Free to be Fabulous* overflows with Debbie's unique vibrancy— it's a powerhouse of tools for maintaining a youthful glow—inside and out. Everything from how to keep your chin from sagging to finding faith for your sagging soul will jump off the pages. If you catch it as it jumps, you'll find yourself a freer, more fabulous you!"

—**Jeanette Levellie**, speaker, humorist, author of *Two Scoops of Grace with Chuckles on Top* and *The Heart of Humor.*

"Practical, encouraging, humorous—*Free to Be Fabulous* gave me hope that the best is yet to be. This is must reading for every woman who believes the lie that she is "over the hill" or fears that day is fast approaching."

—**Marlene Bagnull**, Author

FREE
TO BE
Fabulous

100 Ways to Look and Feel Younger
*—*AT 40, 50 *and* BEYOND*—*

DEBBIE HARDY

New York

FREE TO BE *Fabulous*

100 Ways to Look and Feel Younger at 40, 50 and Beyond

© 2015 DEBBIE HARDY.

Published in New York, New York, by Morgan James Publishing. Morgan James and The Entrepreneurial Publisher are trademarks of Morgan James, LLC.
www.MorganJamesPublishing.com

The Morgan James Speakers Group can bring authors to your live event. For more information or to book an event visit The Morgan James Speakers Group at
www.TheMorganJamesSpeakersGroup.com.

Scripture taken from the HOLY BIBLE, NEW INTERNATIONAL VERSION. Copyright © 1973, 1978, 1984, International Bible Society. Used by permission of Zondervan Bible Publishers.

Quotes available publicly and taken from BrainyQuote.com, LushQuotes.com, Quotationsbook.com, QuoteGarden.com, QuoteWorld.org, WomensHair.About.com

This book and this author present no guarantee that the advice herein will change your life. That's up to you. But it can make you fabulous.

CLEARLY PRINT YOUR NAME ABOVE IN UPPER CASE

Instructions to claim your free eBook edition:
1. Download the BitLit app for Android or iOS
2. Write your name in **UPPER CASE** on the line
3. Use the BitLit app to submit a photo
4. Download your eBook to any device

A free eBook edition is available
with the purchase of this print book.

ISBN 978-1-63047-410-2 paperback
ISBN 978-1-63047-409-6 eBook
ISBN 978-1-63047-411-9 hardcover
Library of Congress Control Number:
2014948992

Cover photos by:
Brian D. Harmon
Bully Curious Productions.

Cover Design by:
Rachel Lopez
www.r2cdesign.com

Interior Design by:
Bonnie Bushman
bonnie@caboodlegraphics.com

In an effort to support local communities and raise awareness and funds, Morgan James Publishing donates a percentage of all book sales for the life of each book to Habitat for Humanity Peninsula and Greater Williamsburg.

Get involved today, visit
www.MorganJamesBuilds.com

Habitat for Humanity®
Peninsula and
Greater Williamsburg
Building Partner

DEDICATION

This book is dedicated to all those who wish
to be fabulous, and those who've already achieved it.

TABLE OF CONTENTS

ACKNOWLEDGEMENTS

Being fabulous can be accomplished alone, but writing a book about it takes a lot of people.

I'd like to thank:

My late husband Bryan, who told me I was fabulous before I was.

Florence Littauer, who encouraged the change in me (read Chapter 1 Step 2 for details).

My nieces Patti, Pamm, and Deanna, fabulous women in their own right, who assured me I was fabulous and built up my self-confidence.

My Brighton (Colorado) Writers Group: Rosalee, Elena, Evelyn, Allison, Patricia, Anne, Tina, Paula, and, Jo who worked with me to polish every suggestion.

Steve Hutson, my agent, who helped every step of the way to publication.

Terry Whalin, my acquisitions editor, who believed in this manuscript from the minute he read the proposal.

My editor and roommate at one of my first writers' conferences, Kathy Ide, who loved my writing and encouraged me to keep at it.

My Fabulous Friends on the cover: (back row) Kathy, Kelly, Elena, and Gene; (middle row) Donna, Dea, Allison, and Brenda; (front row) Glory, Julie, Rosalee, and Dana. We had a Fabulous time at the photo shoot in my living room.

My son Brian Harmon with Bully Curious Productions, who took the cover photo and all my head shots. I hope he realizes his dream of being a cinematographer.

INTRODUCTION

What is fabulous?

- Is it the way you look, making people stop and gawk as you walk by? Not really.
- Maybe it's a beautiful face. No, that part only gets harder as we age. I know. I've tried, but I'll never be Hollywood or Madison-Avenue beautiful.
- Could it be bling on your clothes or in your hair? Uh, no.
- Is it hosting the best parties ever? Not really, although that sounds like fun!
- How about popularity? Well, that could be a benefit of fabulous, but not a definition.

So what is fabulous?

Fabulous is looking great, thinking great, and being a great friend. It's being attractive, but not just your appearance. It's magnetism, being the type of person others want to be around. It's caring about others, using the talents you've been given, and being the best you can be.

Tall order? Not really. Anyone can achieve fabulous. I did. For years I was an unremarkable, frumpy wife and mother. I was a good person, but didn't feel good about myself or my appearance. You'd never tell that by looking at me today. In fact, I look and feel younger than I did 25 years ago!

When you're fabulous, people feel good around you. They want you at their parties, their picnics, their social gatherings. After all, you bring the fun and they notice when you're missing. Also, fabulous people rise above their circumstances and their past hurts. They know that life is a blessing and they live to the fullest.

You can achieve fabulous inside and out with suggestions from this book. You don't need to read it from cover to cover. Just choose what you want to change, and go for it.

There are six sections, all beginning with the letter B. Cute, I know, but they're easy to remember this way:

- **Basics** will give you my story and explain Fabulosity.
- **Beauty** covers outward appearance from head to toe. The chapters are Makeup, Skin, Hair, and Clothing.
- **Beliefs** helps us look at what's going on in our heads and why we do what we do. Chapters are Attitude, Faith, Brain, and Dreams & Wishes.
- **Body** is about what goes on inside, and keeping it working the best it can. These Chapters are Health, Eating, and Exercise.
- **Behavior** includes Relationships, Sleep, and Surroundings.
- **Better You** wraps it all up and ushers you into the world of a new, fabulous you.

Decide what you want to focus on, and work on that. Each day involves doing things with your skin, hair, clothes, and every other topic in here, so you could work on one from each chapter.

I'll start off with my story—how I went from frumpy to fabulous. Then I'll take you through steps to chart your own course to becoming the fabulous person you want to be, the one that's been hiding inside.

A little about me—my regular job is writing and speaking. Topics are:

- Being fabulous
- Letting go of past hurts
- Moving toward your life goals
- Spending smarter for the savvy shopper
- Finding more time in your day and space in your house

Also, I teach at writers' conferences, where I meet with attendees and encourage them in their writing and publishing. My first book, *Stepping Through Cancer: A Guide for the Journey* shares what I learned about caregiving while my husband was dying. I've also written *Steps in Writing and Publishing a Book* for all the would-be authors wanting to fulfill a dream of getting their own books published.

Many others have been through terrible things in their life, and managed to bounce back from them. I like to say that some speakers claim to be resilience experts, but I've been through so much that I am their queen. As Queen of Resilience, I wear a tiara when I speak or teach. That gets people's attention, but being fabulous is what keeps them interested in getting to know me.

Enough about me for now. Ready for a transformation? Let's get started!

Do the one thing you think you cannot do. Fail at it. Try again. Do better the second time. The only people who never tumble are those who never mount the high wire.

This is your moment. Own it.

–Oprah Winfrey

Section 1

BASICS

A girl should be two things: classy and fabulous.
–Coco Chanel

Everybody has sets of "before and after": before and after high school, before and after a wedding, before and after kids, before and after a move, and so on.

Many adults over 40 believe they're past all the "befores" and are living in the "after"-life, so they're done with change. I've heard some folks say, "I've been this way all my life and I'm too old to change, so people will just have to deal with it."

I reply, "Hogwash!" Just as we control what we eat or don't eat, read or don't read, watch or don't watch on TV, we can control many things and transform ourselves, but only if we really want to.

Have you ever met someone who made you feel special just by talking with them? Someone you invite to all your parties because they're so much fun to be around? That's what fabulous is—not something you can take a picture of, but something that makes you feel better about yourself, your life, or the time you spend with them.

This section will explain how I took a dowdy middle-aged woman with a few college credits and morphed her into the vibrant, educated, and self-confident woman I am today. It was simple, but not easy. It required a decision and follow-through, but I did it—and so can you.

If you're dedicated to improving your life, you can make major changes just like me. You can become fabulous at any age!

Let's walk this road together. I've already taken steps and researched paths others have taken, so I'll provide the map. Start with these ideas and branch out from there. If you know another person who has traveled this road, feel free to imitate her (or him). After all, there's more than one way to become fabulous.

The most important thing I can tell you about aging is this: If you really feel that you want to have an off-the-shoulder blouse and some big beads and thong sandals and a dirndl skirt and a magnolia in your hair, do it. Even if you're wrinkled.

–Maya Angelou

Chapter 1

BEFORE I WAS FABULOUS

*The thing I'm the most proud of in my personal life
is that my daughter actually thinks that I'm fabulous.*
–Brooke Shields

I wasn't always fabulous. It's not something I aspired to as a child or a teen, and it didn't seem possible when I was a young adult.

My early childhood was spent living in subsidized housing, commonly called "the projects," where no one was fabulous and I had no hope of ever being so. It was a dreary existence, not something I would wish on anyone.

Then my life changed.

This section will cover my before and after becoming fabulous, and show you how to do the same. Stick with me. You'll be amazed at how you and your life can change.

1. Don't be as old as you used to be.

Anyone who stops learning is old, whether at 20 or 80. Anyone who keeps learning stays young. The greatest thing in life is to keep your mind young.

–Henry Ford

I was an old lady at 39, much older than I am today. No, I'm not like Benjamin Button, the fictional character who lived his life backwards, growing from an old man to a young boy. But in my heart and mind, I really *am* younger than I used to be. And I look it, too.

Back in my late thirties, I was unhappy in my marriage and my career, grossly overweight, insecure, and hiding from the world inside extra-large black and navy-blue garments.

When clothes shopping (which was seldom), I would start with the last size I bought, discover that it didn't fit, have to try on a larger garment, and then go home teary-eyed and empty-handed. Makeup was minimal and I cut my own hair, which was less than flattering. I'll admit it—I was a frumpy old woman.

When I wasn't working at a job I hated, I took care of a home, a husband, a teen and a preteen, resenting the fact that I didn't get to finish my college education. I didn't have, or rather didn't *take*, time for myself. I did just like my mother and so many other women: spent all my time and energy on everyone else and nothing on me.

I had one particularly "ugly day." You know what that is: your makeup looks clownish, your hair has a mind of its own, your clothes don't fit right, and your body feels like it belongs in the hippo exhibit at the zoo. Eventually, I burst into tears.

My loving husband, ever the sensitive one, took me in his arms and asked what the problem was.

Between sobs, everything spilled out in one long sentence: "My-teeth-stick-out,-I'm-fat-,my-clothes-look-horrible,-my-hair-is-a-mess,-I-can't-do-anything-right,and-I'm-ugly." Then I took a breath, waiting for a supportive response.

He looked me in the eye and gently replied, "But you try harder than anyone I know."

Well, that was less than what I had hoped for. But at least it brought a laugh, which I really needed. His comment described what I did all the time: I tried. Didn't succeed at much of anything, but I definitely tried.

Compare that to today. I am many years older but not nearly as heavy. I've earned two college degrees, am an author and a public speaker, and have self-confidence. I wear brightly-colored clothing and I like what I see in the mirror. I look and feel fabulous and secure in who I am.

What made the difference?

I did the laundry. No, really! I did the laundry.

As I was folding clothes one day, I held up a pair of my sturdy white cotton briefs and was instantly transported to childhood, when my sister and I would fold the family's laundry. We held up a pair of Mom's underwear and laughed hysterically. They were *huge!* And now, here I was, holding up that same huge pair of underwear. Well, not literally the same pair, but they looked the same and were just as big as Mom's.

That was my "Aha! moment." I realized I was becoming my mother and I was thinking, acting, and looking much older than my age.

My family has a history of dying young, mostly from weight-related illnesses and heart problems, things that are preventable. Understanding how similar I was to my mother shook me to the core. She never finished high school, had her first heart attack at the age of 49, and died fourteen years later after many surgeries and hospital stays. Dreading the same fate, I decided not to let that happen to me.

First, I enrolled in night courses at a Christian college near our home. My employer had a tuition-reimbursement program, so it would cost me only time and effort to get that elusive degree.

Then I went shopping, but not for the conservative clothes I normally bought. This time, I was looking for pretty underwear, something Mom would never have worn. I wanted lovely, lacy, and (dare I say it?) sexy undergarments to replace those briefs and functional old-lady bras.

What happened was not just a clothing change but an attitude shift. Wearing something lacy close to my skin made me feel pretty and confident. I developed a positive outlook that I had only been faking up to that point.

That mindset ingrained itself in me and expanded into other areas of my life. I acted like I knew what I was at college, and my classmates and professors began asking for my input. I started wearing splashes of color to brighten my dark wardrobe. I copied makeup from magazines and had my hair cut professionally into a modern style.

Because I was feeling better, I began to smile and laugh more. And since I no longer needed food for comfort, I lost weight.

A few years later, I became single again (not a result of the "try harder" remark, by the way). In my forties, I remarried and the wedding photographer asked my two sisters which one was my mother. That remark made them angry but made me smile. My new choices had made me younger.

After Bryan and I married, we discussed how we'd like to see the other person change. I was miffed when Bryan said he'd like me to have a closer walk with the Lord. I attended church most of my life and had raised my boys in the church. What could he possibly mean?

But as I began to spend regular time reading my Bible and praying, I learned what a real relationship with God can be. That changed not only how I spent my mornings, but also my attitude toward others and my patience with the world.

I finally discovered what truly fabulous people know: beauty comes from within and starts with the right attitude. All the rest of the stuff, what you see on the outside, is the shell that houses the real beauty. And just because you're aging, you don't need to look or feel old.

2. Fabulous is simple, but not easy.

I wish I could just go tell all the young women I work with, all these fabulous women, "Believe in yourself and negotiate for yourself. Own your own success." I wish I could tell that to my daughter. But it's not that simple.

–Sheryl Sandberg

If you read my Table of Contents, you may think that it looks too easy to make a difference in your life. That was done intentionally. I don't want you to give up before you start.

When I was a teenager, I perused magazines with pictures of beautiful women and wished I could look like them. For a day or two after every televised beauty pageant, I strutted around the house, pretending to have a crown on my head. But as a plain, pimply-faced fat girl, all I could do was dream.

When I became a woman, I resigned myself to being a plain-Jane church lady, with nothing to make me stand out from the crowd. I figured I'd end up looking just like my mother.

Then I read a book by Florence Littauer called *It Takes So Little to Be Above Average*. Florence made it clear that we can easily be above average in many areas.

I was sure I could never be more than average in appearance, so I decided to be an above-average mom, wife, employee, musician, and everything else.

At times it was difficult not to settle for average, especially in mundane things like mowing my lawn or driving a car. And I probably made it more difficult than it needed to be. But I achieved the results I was seeking.

I hope that, by reading this book, you'll discover ways to be fabulous without working as hard as I did.

3. Fabulosity 101

> *Somebody who can reckon with the past, who can live with the past*
> *in the present, and move towards the future—that's fabulous.*
> **–Bruce Springsteen**

Free to be Fabulous contains practical ideas to incorporate into your life. Some may work for you and others may not. Take what you like and discard the rest.

There are no magic pills, super cosmetics, or enchanted secrets here, just ideas. They may be "secret" in that you haven't heard of them before, but there's nothing extraordinary about them. No expensive lotions or super creams and definitely no drastic changes like plastic surgery or injections. Most of these ideas are just common sense.

It can take 21 days or longer to make or change a habit. So pick one and try it every day for three weeks to see if it works for you. Once it's ingrained, move on to another suggestion. At that rate, you could make seventeen changes in the next year. Talk about a makeover!

If you read an idea or try one and decide you don't like it, no problem. Any change is up to you, so don't feel pressured. This is an individual journey. Choose your own steps.

Since it's much easier, quicker and more noticeable to others if you change the outside, you might want to start with the Beauty and Body sections. Changes inside, like attitude and emotions, take longer to show themselves, but they can be the most satisfying. Do whatever feels right for you and have fun along the way.

This is an exciting ride. I should know—I've been on this journey for over 20 years and I'm still finding ways to improve. There's always some area that needs work. That's humbling but oh so rewarding.

I hope you'll muster the courage to hop on this ride and enjoy yourself. I think you'll be pleased with the result.

Make the most of yourself ... for that is all there is of you.
–Ralph Waldo Emerson

Section 2

BEAUTY

The pursuit of truth and beauty is a sphere of activity in which we are permitted to remain children all our lives.
–Albert Einstein

When I became engaged at college in Ohio, my fiancé had already met my family, who lived just a few hours away. But I hadn't yet met his family in Colorado. He arranged a ride for me with some female classmates who were driving cross-country after Christmas.

Since it would be a 26-hour trip, I knew my makeup and hairdo wouldn't last. So instead of getting all dolled up and retouching it at every pit stop, I put my hair in curlers, covered it with a knit cap, and left my face naked. I figured I would "make myself beautiful" somewhere in the last few miles.

When we stopped for lunch, I overheard some truckers talking as I returned from the restroom. One said, "Well, either it's a very pretty boy or an awful ugly girl."

Hearing that comment made me feel unattractive, so I went back to the restroom, took the curlers out, combed my hair, and put on some makeup. Although I'd never see those guys again, I felt I needed to prove that I could be pretty, not just an ugly girl.

I've since learned that beauty is really being proud of who you are. Makeup, hair, and clothing only augment what God gave you.

First Peter 3:3-4 tells us:

Your beauty should not come from outward adornment, such as elaborate hairstyles and the wearing of gold jewelry or fine clothes. Rather, it should be that of your inner self, the unfading beauty of a gentle and quiet spirit, which is of great worth in God's sight.

If you're like me, you probably feel more confident and secure when you enhance your natural beauty. Fortunately, it's not difficult to improve our appearance.

We're able to change the way we look, think, act, and feel by honestly considering what we can improve and doing something about it. The changes in this book can become permanent if you make them a part of your life.

Our main goal is to be the best, the most fabulous we can be. Let's go!

Chapter 2

MAKEUP

The best thing is to look natural, but it takes makeup to look natural.
–Calvin Klein

My pale skin is less than flattering. In fact, if I go anywhere without makeup, I feel like people are staring at me, and not because I look good.

When I first started using makeup, I only emphasized my features: mascara to open my eyes, a little blush on the cheeks, and a wisp of lipstick. It was easy to apply and helped my self-confidence. After a while, I decided that my face needed more, so I added foundation and eye colors. These little touches made me feel attractive, and gave me a reason to smile as I entered a room.

Another good reason for makeup is that you can look healthy even when you're not feeling well. I had an upset stomach last week and, with puffy eyes and red splotches from chin to hairline, I looked exactly like I felt: lousy. Unfortunately, I had a speaking engagement and couldn't hide at home. A thicker foundation covered the splotches on my face and gave me the color that I lacked. When I added blush, eye shadow, liner, and mascara, I no longer looked sick.

Makeup is an individual choice, not only how much and what colors but how often you use it. For me, it never fails—when I decide to spend the day at home without makeup, that's when someone invites me to lunch with a half-hour notice. So I "put on my face" every day. It makes me feel more confident and I've found that I actually get more work done.

Using makeup is like wearing pretty underwear. Your self-esteem shouldn't depend on it, but you may feel better with it. I know I do. Makeup should enhance your confidence, not determine it.

Below are some ideas to help emphasize your good features, deemphasize those you're not crazy about, and build up your confidence in the process. Try them a little at a time so you're not shocked by the transformation.

1. Apply foundation to cover flaws and put your best face forward.

Makeup is different for every person. Everyone has a different feature on their face that they like to show off.

–Lauren Conrad

No one has perfect skin. Even most models have to cover up imperfections and emphasize some features to look beautiful. Cindy Crawford has often said, "Even I don't look like Cindy Crawford in the morning."

As we age, we can get darker spots on our cheeks and rings under our eyes. Some ladies may have a noticeable birthmark or may develop spots of skin with no pigmentation. But it's easy to even out skin tones with foundation.

When I was a teen, my parents wouldn't allow me to use makeup, so I hid it in my purse and applied it when I arrived wherever I was going. Once, I was sitting behind my dad in the car on the way to church, putting on makeup using his rear-view mirror. Unfortunately, Mom caught me and yelled, "What do you think you're doing?"

I was too embarrassed to reply, "Improving my appearance." Instead, I said the usual, "I don't know." I hid my makeup better after that.

Even though we no longer have teen acne to worry about or need to hide our makeup from our parents, we may wamt to cover imperfections so we can be more beautiful. Foundation gives an even skin tone and concealer covers the occasional flaw.

I saw a commercial about makeup for men, mostly to hide flaws and dark circles. The announcer called it "camouflage" so guys wouldn't feel emasculated using it. Maybe it should be called "Camou-flaws" since it was intended to disguise facial flaws. By the way, I only saw that commercial once, so I have no idea who made it. Guess it wasn't as big a seller as they had hoped.

There's no shame in using makeup. In fact, people today have come to expect it, especially on women. If you've never used it, try it before you decide.

2. Use foundation that's slightly lighter or darker than your skin.

I love the confidence that makeup gives me.
–Tyra Banks

Many people believe that tanned skin looks beautiful. It might, but it will look unnatural if your face is a different color from the rest of you. Instead of rubbing a tan on just your face, go with foundation the same color as your skin or one shade lighter or darker. That way, you won't look like you have someone else's head stuck on your body. A perfectly-made-up face with a line along the jaw separating it from a lighter or darker neck looks unnatural. It's much better to have the same color from forehead to neckline.

If you're blessed with naturally bronzed skin, you'll probably need less makeup. You may want to even out your tone to make your face appear flawless or touch up a little imperfection. Look in a mirror critically to see where you could improve.

Your skin color may darken or lighten as you spend more or less time outside, so alter your makeup to match the season. Use a darker shade for summer and lighter for winter. During spring and fall, put a little of both shades of liquid foundation on the back of your hand, mix them, and then apply to your face. You can add more dark or light depending on how pale or tanned you've become.

Makeup can accumulate in the creases of your skin, especially in wrinkles. One way to prevent this is to dab it on lightly. Another is to add a dusting of face powder, which can set the foundation and keep it where you want it.

Ironically, the trick is to apply makeup to not look made up. Your face is the canvas on which to paint.

3. Apply mascara to open up your eyes.

Makeup is scary. When I do it myself, it's just mascara, and sometimes I forget even to do that.
–Sandra Bullock

My son was born with long, dark, curly eyelashes. Decades later, he still has them. Most people aren't that lucky, including me. But thanks to thin lips and a "cute little button nose," my eyes are my best feature, so I apply mascara every day.

You may be tempted to buy the blackest shade available. I wouldn't recommend that, except for evening or occasions when you want a dramatic look. Dark mascara can smudge and give you raccoon eyes. And having that kind of impact all the time gives you nowhere to expand when you want to look even better.

Instead, for everyday use, try a shade that's a little darker than your hair. And use waterproof if you think you might be crying. Black streaks down the cheeks are not pretty on anyone.

When I was going through a rough time in my life, my mascara would run when I cried, which was often. I had my beautician dye my lashes so I wouldn't need mascara. The process took about 20 minutes and lasted several months. The color didn't flake, run, or rub off. Dyeing might also be good if you're going on your honeymoon or somewhere you want to look gorgeous day and night.

If you're not blessed with eyelashes that curl naturally, use a lash curler. Use it before applying mascara, or your lashes may be brittle and break when you squeeze them.

Be sure the curler is in good working order. I heard of a lady who lost one of the cushions from her curler but used it anyway. Instead of curling the lashes on her right eye, she snipped them off! She could have snipped off the left set of lashes to match and waited until they grew back. Instead, she learned how to apply false eyelashes to both eyes.

I guess there's always a silver lining—and more than one way to use makeup to your advantage.

4. Get a hands-on makeover.

I love sitting in the makeup trailer and getting my makeup done in 15 minutes as opposed to an hour and a half.
–Claire Danes

Remember the TV show *Rhoda*? The title character was played by Valerie Harper, with Julie Kavner as her sister Brenda.

On one episode, when Brenda walked in, she was beautiful! Absolutely stunning, drop-dead gorgeous. The studio audience reacted with "oohs" and "aahs" and applause. Brenda told Rhoda she'd gone to a department store for a makeover, after which she had purchased every product the saleslady used on her face.

Brenda then put two huge shopping bags on the table with all the items she bought, costing hundreds of dollars. She said, "I have all this stuff, but I have no idea what to do with it."

That's the problem. A makeover at the mall or a department store can make you look beautiful, but if someone else does all the work, you probably won't know how to duplicate it when you get home. Watching someone else apply makeup to your face isn't the same as doing it yourself. And it doesn't give you the confidence you'll need to do it every morning.

Instead, get a makeover where you paint your own face. Some makeup companies like Mary Kay host makeover events. Each lady gets her own mirror along with makeup products to match her skin and eye colors. Since she applies it herself, she can recreate the look at home.

My friend Donna (she's on the cover) is a Mary Kay representative and hosted a party like this. We all brought snacks and beverages and had a great time. We took "before" and "after" pictures of everyone so each lady could see how much better she looked with makeup she applied following the expert's advice. We even had feather boas, sequined tops, and other fun accessories to glamorize ourselves for the photographs. The event gave us lots of memories along with the knowledge and ability to make ourselves beautiful every day.

After your face looks exactly the way you want it, buy the products you used during your makeover. It's easier to copy the appearance if you use the same merchandise. When you need to replenish your supply, buy it from the same representative. If that's not an option, take the used-up package to a store and find something that matches closely.

5. Apply makeup in natural light.

I find most men don't like a lot of makeup.
–Chloe Sevigny

You can spend hours in front of your bathroom mirror applying makeup until you look stunning. Then you go outside and your face looks yellow or gray or orange. Artificial lights can give your skin a tint that seems perfect, but under natural light, the real color comes through.

Some lighted makeup mirrors have a variety of settings so you can see what your face will look like in the sun or under different lights. If you don't have one of those, apply your makeup, and then take a mirror outside and look at yourself. When you're pleased with the results, go with it. Otherwise, change the color until it suits you.

Trying out makeup in a department store is no help. Those bright fluorescent bulbs are intended to make everything sparkle and shine. And at some makeup counters, the salespeople have you put foundation on the back of your hand to find a match. My hand is much lighter than my face, so that doesn't work for me.

When I was a teen, I saved my pennies and bought my first bottle of liquid foundation. I was so excited! I went straight home and applied it, then gasped when I saw the tan makeup streaked on my pale skin. It was totally wrong. I took it back to the store, but the salesperson wouldn't refund my money. So I had to save some more to buy the right shade.

To find the best foundation for you, test a small spot on your cheek, then go outside into natural light. Take a friend with you who will tell you the truth. Don't buy a large container of makeup until you're certain it's the right shade.

You can save money by buying makeup when it goes on sale or ends up in a clearance bin. Just make sure it's the right color. If your exact brand and shade are on sale, be thankful and get it. Even if it's a shade lighter or darker, it may be worth getting a few dollars off.

6. Color your eyelids.

If you're wearing smoky eye makeup, a little beige or gold pencil on the inner eye corners will open up the area, but you only want to do it if the shadow is really dark. Otherwise, light pencil makes your eyes look too far apart, like a fish.

–Gisele Bundchen

When I was a young woman, eye shadow was always blue. Later, eye shadow needed to match your clothes, so you had to buy a rainbow. There was also a time when eye shadow was supposed to match your eye color. How boring is that?

Now, you can use whatever colors you like and apply them as dark as you want. But when you try something new, get someone else's opinion. I can't tell you how many times I thought I looked pretty good, and then realized that people noticed me for the wrong reason.

Since I'm a widow now, I don't have a husband at home to give me his opinion. So I tend to stay with the same colors and blend everything really well. After I back out of the garage, I stop and check my face in the rear-view mirror to see how it looks in natural light.

Then I remind myself of Ecclesiastes 3:11, which says, "He has made everything beautiful in its time." And that includes you and me. We're beautiful.

7. Apply eyeliner to look natural.

The sweetest thing a guy said is that I look
pretty with or without makeup.
–Vanessa Hudgens

Have you ever seen a woman with eyeliner so dark you can't help but stare at her? The effect is dramatic and attention-catching, but it screams, "I'm wearing face paint!" To be really beautiful, a woman's makeup should *emphasize* her features, not *overshadow* them.

Liner can be applied with pencil and smudged, or as a liquid for a cleaner look. Either way, taper the ends so there's no obvious start or finish to the line. You don't want to look like you used a Magic Marker to underline (or over-line) your eyes.

Take a crack at different colors to see which works best. Brown eyes can look alluring with blue liner, and green accentuates hazel eyes. You may want to have an assortment of colors to vary your look depending on how you feel.

If you want something more permanent, you could have the liner tattooed on. However, let me offer several warnings about that:

- It hurts! I've never had the nerve to try it, but a friend at work had it done, and she said she hadn't cried like that in years.
- The liner may not fade with time. Imagine your grandmother with dark lines around her eyes. That's what you could look like in a few years.
- Styles change. One woman I know had "cat's-eye" liner tattooed on her lids, with the outer edges curled up. That may have been great in the sixties, but her eyes just look weird now.

Try different techniques and stick with what works for you. Change with the styles if you want, but make sure you're comfortable and confident with your choice.

8. Tweeze your eyebrows.

> *Just because you want to be glamorous,*
> *don't be a sheep about your makeup.*
> **–Loretta Young**

One way to emphasize your eyes is to shape your brows. Using tweezers to pull out one hair at a time may hurt a bit, but you won't need to do it often.

Plucking under the brows, not above, will raise the brow line and make your eyes appear more open. Get rid of more hairs toward the sides of your face so your brows taper down.

If you've never tweezed before, pluck just a few hairs from above each eye, doing your best to keep the brows even. Then pluck some more in a couple of hours or days. That way it won't hurt so much or make your eyes red and puffy.

A trick to cut down on the pain is to put baby teething gel like Orajel™ on your brows to deaden the nerves before you tweeze. And apply a cold washcloth or an icepack briefly after to reduce any possible swelling.

To get a good idea of what the finished product should look like, notice brows in ads for products other than makeup. Try different styles until you find one that works best for you.

It used to be the style to have very thin lines or to shave the entire brow and then pencil it in. The "let it all hang out" era of the sixties encouraged everyone to go natural and eyebrows were left to their own bushy devices. I'm sure glad we've come to our senses.

Remember that your eyebrows are sisters, not twins. They don't need to be mirror images of each other. Don't measure them to be sure they're exactly the same, like a coworker did. Just have your brows match so they look like they belong on the same face.

Also, don't tweeze right before you go to a special event or get your picture taken, and definitely not right before your wedding. Try to pluck at least one day ahead so any puffiness or redness will have time to fade. You may not have a bad reaction, but it's better to be safe than have pictures with red, puffy eyes.

You can also have your eyebrows professionally shaped by waxing, which can be painful or threading, which is faster than tweezing. But be prepared to pay for the convenience of not doing it yourself.

9. Beware of clown face.

I feel more confident if my makeup looks good.
–Ellie Goulding

As a woman ages and her eyesight fails, she may apply makeup more heavily so she can see it. Older ladies often end up with little red circles on their cheeks and eyes outlined with dark pencil. All they need is a blue wig and a red nose and they're ready for the circus!

When my eyes aged, I got a super-magnifying mirror. That way I didn't need to exaggerate my colors or paint the eyeliner darker to see it.

A lot of eye shadow comes with diagrams and application suggestions. You can also search the internet or get a magazine with pictures and instructions. Keep them handy when you apply the color, especially the first few times.

Always blend carefully, and don't overdo it.

Practice at home when you don't have to go anywhere. If you're not comfortable with the results, you can wash it off and start over. But if you look fabulous, go somewhere to show off.

While you want to avoid "clown face," don't be afraid of color. Start with pastels for your eyes and cheeks. Once you get accustomed to color on your face, you can become more dramatic with darker shades.

After not being allowed to wear makeup as a teenager, I eased my way into it as an adult. Now, I use whatever colors I want, and it's fun.

10. Remove your makeup every night.

Dear face wash commercials - Nobody actually splashes their face with water like that. Sincerely, my bathroom floor is wet.
–Author Unknown

Most teens know that washing off their makeup eliminates clogged pores. But if you're past the age of acne, going to bed with makeup on your face is still not good for your skin's health. Besides the possibility of those clogged pores, rubbing your face on your pillow all night can irritate your skin and stain your linens.

After one of *those* days, I didn't have the patience to wait for the water in my bathroom sink to warm up so I could wash my makeup off. A cold splash in the face at night would revive me and I wouldn't be able fall asleep. So I just tissued off what I could and went to bed. But I paid for it in the morning. I woke up with smudges under my eyes, stains on my pillowcase, and an angry spot on my face. So now, instead of waiting till the last minute, I wash and moisturize an hour before bedtime so it won't interfere with my rest.

I once worked with a lady who always wanted to look her best for her husband, so she never let him see her natural self. She would go to bed with makeup on. After her husband fell asleep, she'd get out of bed, remove her makeup, wash and moisturize her face, and then go back to bed. In the morning, she'd arise an hour early to reapply her makeup and do her hair before he awakened.

She thought this was the best way of both looking beautiful for her husband and exercising good skin care. It did keep her face clean and healthy, but it didn't help the honesty in their marriage. She had a beautiful complexion when they divorced.

I don't recommend that you follow this example, since your husband needs to see you as you really are, imperfections and all. But that needn't keep you from looking your best most of the time.

11. Smile with your eyes and your teeth.

Your smile will give you a positive countenance that will make people feel comfortable around you.
–Les Brown

When I teach my Fabulous workshop, I have the ladies in the room pair up and look at each other with expressionless faces. No curling of the lips into either a smile or a sneer. Most of them have trouble *not* smiling or laughing, but I urge them to take this exercise seriously.

Once they've settled down, I tell them to smile with their just eyes, relaxing those muscles, and raising their eyebrows. The ladies are always amazed at how this softens their faces and makes them appear more welcoming and friendly. Usually, they break into a grin and start talking and laughing.

That sober face is how people see us much of the time. One family member was looking at pictures taken at a birthday party. In every one of her photos, she had a scowl on her face. She turned to me and asked, "Do I really look like that?" It broke my heart to tell her she did. She wasn't really a crabby person, but her face said otherwise.

Look at yourself in a mirror with your facial muscles relaxed. That is what folks see when they look at you. Without a smile, no one would have an idea that you're a warm, friendly person. That look will keep people away, leaving you isolated.

Now, raise your brows slightly and smile at your reflection using only your eyes. Notice how your face appears friendlier and more inviting. This is the face you want others to see—the one where you look approachable and eager to be a friend.

Next, smile with your lips closed and then again with them parted slightly. See the difference. A smile with closed lips is a courteous smile. One with lips parted exudes friendliness and openness.

Some women may feel self-conscious about their teeth. Most people won't notice if your teeth are straight or crooked, white or yellow, present or AWOL. However, they will notice if you're hesitant about your smile or cover your mouth with your hand. And that will very likely cause them to stare more, which you probably wanted to avoid in the first place.

Create a smile by thinking of something or someone you love. It's hard not to smile when I think about my grandkids, music, or moose tracks ice cream. Any one of those will bring a grin to my face and a sparkle to my eyes.

Smiling with your eyes and your teeth will give you a twinkle … and maybe a new friend, a new relationship, or a new love.

Chapter 3

SKIN

My skin may have wrinkles but it's because I'm smiling so much.
–Olivia Williams

*L*ike many teenagers, I had zits. Still had pimples in my twenties. I tried all sorts of treatments, but only time resolved the problem for me. Time and a move to a drier climate.

I grew up along the banks of Lake Erie, where oily skin and high humidity were a way of life. I didn't use moisturizer, since my skin never completely dried out. Our towels and sheets never dried out either, but that's another story.

My husband and I relocated to Colorado when I was 25 and that nasty acne *finally* cleared up. I was thrilled to get rid of it. But the dry air presented another dilemma: dry, flaky, itchy skin. Not just on my face but all over my body. I became good friends with Ivory® soap and Jergens® lotion.

Since I needed to seal in moisture after washing my face, applying cream or lotion was absolutely necessary. I tried store-brand moisturizers. All of them made my skin dewy, but they also brought back those dreaded zits. I discovered that if I tissued off the excess, I got the benefit of the lotion without clogging my pores.

After using moisturizer for decades, my skin now makes me look younger than my chronological age. In fact, I've been "carded" at several restaurants when I asked for the senior discount. What a great feeling, having to get out my driver's license to prove how old I am!

Since our skin is the largest organ in our bodies, we need to take care of it, so it can protect all the other organs. Here are some suggestions to help your skin look younger.

1. Moisturize, moisturize, moisturize.

> *No matter how late it is, when I get home, I take the time to clean and moisturize my face.*
>
> **–Demi Moore**

The three most important things in real estate are location, location, and location. Similarly, there are three secrets to younger-looking skin: moisturize, moisturize, and moisturize. It's that important.

After you wash your face every morning and evening, lightly buff it dry with a towel to remove oils and dirt, then apply a moisturizing lotion or cream. If your face feels greasy, use a tissue and wipe off the excess.

Also apply a moisturizer over your entire body after you bathe or shower. Be sure to rub it into your elbows and knees, where you can easily develop dry, calloused skin.

If you live in an area with enough humidity to keep your skin supple, you could probably get away with less lotion. In the winter or any other time your skin gets a little dryer, purchase a more expensive brand to get better results. Those of us who live in a dry climate would benefit greatly from spending a few more pennies. It's worth it for me.

One warning if you want to use scented lotion. Apply it only from the neck down. I once used peach lotion on my face. It smelled great, but the scent created a problem. Everything I ate that day had a peachy taste to it—even my ham sandwich at lunch. Not a taste sensation I want to repeat.

And if you do use scented lotion, coordinate it with your perfume or cologne. You don't want to be a walking fruit basket or a French garden.

2. Rub upward to keep muscles from sagging.

My skin care routine is very easy, I wash my face religiously. When you wear a lot of make-up like I do it's so important to really super-clean your face so your pores are open.
–Heidi Klum

For years, I heard when drying your face or applying moisturizer, you should rub in the direction that your facial hair grows, which would be downward. I followed that advice, but my muscles moved in the direction they were pushed and I developed jowls. Yes, jowls! That sagging on either side of the jaw that you usually see only on dogs or grouchy old people.

I couldn't bear the thought of my cheeks brushing my shoulders, so I changed how I rubbed my face. I gently pushed my cheeks and jowls up with the towel every morning and night. After a while, my jowls disappeared and now my facial muscles don't sag nearly as much.

This is true for other areas of your body as well. When you towel off after a shower or bath, try rubbing your skin gently upward instead of down. Doing the same when you apply body lotion just might help reduce saggy knees and the appearance of cellulite on your thighs.

3. Moisturize your neck.

> *My husband gave me a necklace. It's fake. I requested fake. Maybe I'm paranoid, but in this day and age, I don't want something around my neck that's worth more than my head.*
> **–Rita Rudner**

Do you know where wrinkles typically appear first? Not your face or hands, where sunscreen and moisturizer are regularly applied, but on your neck.

I know a beautiful middle-aged lady who has not one wrinkle on her face. Yet her neck looks like elephant legs. No kidding—she has more wrinkles on her neck than laundry left in the dryer. Why? She moisturizes faithfully, using many of the latest products, but stops at her jawline.

Moisturize your neck every time you put lotion on your face. Again, rub upward gently to keep the muscles from sagging. And continue down into the V that sometimes shows above your neckline. If too dry, your chest skin can look crêpe-y—like crêpe paper, with annoying little crinkles. You want people to notice your beautiful face, not the wrinkles on or below your neck.

4. Slather on the sunscreen.

> *I protect my skin with sunscreen and am religious about keeping my face moisturized and properly protected all day, so I also use a face lotion with SPF 30.*
> **–Amanda Beard**

If you cook a steak too long or at too high a temperature, it becomes tough and leathery, right? Same for your skin.

Many people have melanomas removed because they were too vain to use a little protection. It's one of the most common and preventable forms of cancer, so why put yourself in danger? Sunscreen is not just for kids. I know it's a hassle to apply and reapply when it washes or sweats off, but it's absolutely necessary.

If your skin is dark, don't think that you won't get burned.[1] Having more melanin doesn't mean that you're immune to sun damage. You wouldn't leave cookies in the oven for an extra half hour just because they're already browned. In the same way, you need to protect yourself no matter what color your skin is.

Choose sunscreen with an SPF of at least 30. And no, putting SPF 15 on twice doesn't count.

One dermatologist I know applies sunscreen to his entire body after every shower. Many of his patients' skin cancers were in areas that clothing would normally cover. So wearing long sleeves or slacks did not guarantee them protection.

And don't forget your lips. They can be damaged by the sun as well.

5. Avoid the sun as much as possible.

To sit in the shade on a fine day and look upon verdure [lush plants] is the most perfect refreshment.
–Jane Austen

One easy way to reduce your chance of wrinkles and skin cancer is to stay out of the sun.

If you live in a sunny state like I do, that may be difficult. You might need to invest in a canopy for when you attend your kids' and grandkids' games. And it's no shame to use an umbrella when it's not raining. Shade is the ultimate sunscreen, and an umbrella is a lot cooler than long sleeves and long pants to cover your skin.

My son Tim knew this before he even went to kindergarten. A family cruise to Mexico included a day on the beach at Playa del Carmen. While Mom, Dad, and Brother frolicked in the waves, fair-skinned Tim sat in the shade of a beached rowboat, playing in the sand.

At the time, I was upset that he wasn't taking advantage of the chance to splash in the Gulf of Mexico. I made him stand in knee-deep water so I could take a picture. As soon as he heard the camera click, he headed back to his shade.

That night, while I was up applying aloe vera to everyone else's sunburn, Tim slept contentedly.

When my boys had Field Day in elementary school, other parents laughed when I showed up with an umbrella on a sunny day. But while they were burning and dripping with sweat, I was sitting pretty in my personal shade. Many of them told me wished they had brought an umbrella. The next year, they did!

If you can, find a tree to hide under. That's one reason God created them. Might as well take advantage of shade already in place if you didn't bring your own.

6. Treat yourself to a manicure or a pedicure.

I should get a manicure more often.
–Savannah Guthrie

An easy and inexpensive extravagance is to treat yourself to a manicure, a pedicure, or both, even if you do it yourself. You can feel so feminine with your nails shiny and colorful. Invite a friend over so you can paint each other's nails and giggle. My granddaughters and I do this every time they visit, and we all look forward to it.

If you're new to manicures, begin with a shade close to your skin color. After you become adept at it, try darker or brighter shades. When the polish ends up on the skin around your nails, use the thumbnail from your other hand to clean it up, just like a manicurist does.

I remember as a teen watching the movie "Funny Girl" with Barbra Streisand. The filmmakers didn't want to bring attention to Barbra's long, signature fingernails, so they painted them a color to match her skin tone. As a result, her fingers looked long, thin, and elegant. Ever since then, I've always had a bottle of similar nail polish.

Sometimes I want color on my hands (like purple when I'm going to a Colorado Rockies baseball game), and other times I just want a finished look. That's when I grab the neutral polish. I still love it, especially when I'm traveling and don't want to worry about touching up chipped nails or spilling nail polish in my suitcase.

And don't forget your feet. Fill a small dish tub or pot with warm water and stir in liquid soap. Use it to soak your hands and feet, and scrub off dead skin cells prior to painting your nails. Then let gorgeous toes peek out from sandals or open-toed shoes.

A friend of mine, when her sister comes to visit, fills her jetted bathtub with warm water and adds lavender-scented Epsom salts. The two of them sit on the side with their feet in the water while they chat. Then they give each other a pedicure. It's a girls' day at the spa without the spa price.

Polishing your nails is one habit you won't need to do every day. The color on your fingers may start to wear or chip after just a few days, especially if you use your hands for housework, gardening, filing, or other tasks. When you use a polish the same color as your skin, wearing or chipping off isn't as noticeable, so your manicure could last longer. But a pedicure can last a week or two, if not more.

Once you get used to having polished nails, you may feel naked without them. So take a half hour and paint them. Besides making your hands beautiful, it will give you time to just sit and do nothing while you wait for them to dry. If you're like me, you need an excuse to not work so hard.

7. Soften your feet, especially your heels.

> *How beautiful your sandaled feet,*
> *O prince's daughter!*
> *Your graceful legs are like jewels,*
> *the work of an artist's hands.*
> **–Song of Solomon 7:1**

Sometimes our feet can get dry and cracked, especially in summer when we wear sandals and flip-flops. I once saw a video of a woman whose husband used his power sander to smooth her heels. A little drastic, if you ask me, and unsafe, too.

But there's an easier solution. When you're getting ready for bed, wash and dry your feet, then slather them with petroleum jelly like Vaseline®. Put on a pair of cotton socks to keep the goo in place and so your sheets don't get greasy. When you wake in the morning, you'll be surprised at how much softer your feet are. Repeat this as often as necessary, which may be several nights if your feet have been neglected for too long.

Some people have told me, "I can't wear socks to bed. I won't be able to sleep." If that's you, find another six hours or so when you can wear socks. Since I'd rather wear my sandals in the daytime and socks at night, I just turn on the ceiling fan to keep cool.

Giving your feet some Tender Loving Care can help them feel better, look better, and keep you in better "standing."

8. Don't wait to lose weight.

The older you get, the tougher it is to lose weight,
because by then your body and your fat are really good friends.
–Author Unknown

My friend Rosalee (she's on the cover) waited until her seventies to lose 50 pounds and now has sagging skin. Muscle tone below the surface can reduce the sagging, so Rosalee is now working out regularly. She is tightening up, but it has taken a long time. It's better if you exercise while you're losing the weight, so your body can adapt.

The longer you put off losing weight, the harder it will be. As we age, our skin isn't as elastic as it used to be and may not shrink to our new body size, leaving unsightly sags. But if you drop weight slowly, your skin has time to reduce with less sag. And losing the weight slowly will increase the likelihood of keeping it off.

I was once on a fad diet of only hormones and 500 calories of food every day. I lost a lot of weight, but could only use the diet a few weeks at a time. In between, I maintained the weight as my skin gradually shrunk to its new size. Unfortunately, when I resumed eating normally, my body resumed its customary weight. But it didn't have sagging or stretched skin to contend with.

Eating less isn't easy, so we tend to put it off, like delaying a visit to the dentist. If you're like me, you want to wait until after … that special dinner, next week, January 1st, or whenever.

Instead, start today.

Proper skin care is one of the most important things you can do to look younger. And following these simple steps can make it easy.

I'm a big believer in that if you focus on good skin care, you really won't need a lot of makeup.

–Demi Moore

Chapter 4

HAIR

Does not the very nature of things teach you that ... if a woman has long hair, it is her glory?
–1 Corinthians 11:14, 15

I love long hair. My face does not, so I can't let my hair grow. I'm jealous of friends and actresses with long, flowing locks that sway in the breeze. I wish I could look like that, but my cheeks seem chubbier when my hair falls below the jawline. I need height on my head, so in order to look good with long hair, I'd need it short on top, which would be a mullet. Not a good look for me.

As a teenager, I tried to copy the Beatles style of long straight hair with bangs. Since my hair was naturally curly, having that style involved more than just brushing. I raided the kitchen for large juice cans to set my hair. My hair wasn't totally straight, but it was a lot less curly. My bangs wouldn't fit around a can, so I taped them to my forehead to keep them straight. I have no idea how I slept like that!

As an adult, long hair made me look older, so I settled for a pixie-ish cut. Bryan, my second husband, asked me to let my hair grow. After a while, my hair was down past my shoulders. He enjoyed running his hands through it, but didn't like the way it looked. He told me, even suggested, that I should cut it.

We did compromise, though—I found a 15-inch-long fall that matched my hair color. I kept that in my nightstand, so when my husband wanted long hair spread on my pillow, I could accommodate him. It worked like a charm!

Here are some ideas to have the crowning glory you deserve.

1. Keep your hairstyle current.

> *If you look over the years, the styles have changed—the clothes, the hair, the production, the approach to the songs. The icing to the cake has changed flavors. But if you really look at the cake itself, it's really the same.*

> **–John Oates**

A lady I know received compliments on her high school senior picture, so she's maintained the same style for years. Unfortunately, that look is aging her. Another friend's stylist talked her into updating her 'do. Her hair looked different when she left the shop, but the next morning, she styled it the same as she had before.

So how do you find a new hairstyle? Check pictures online or in magazines for one you like that wouldn't be too difficult for you to do every morning. Take it to your stylist and ask him or her to copy it.

Let your beautician know how you'd like to look, especially if it's a little different from the photo. If you're not happy with the results, have the stylist keep working at it until you're pleased.

Be flexible with your request. Sometimes your stylist can't duplicate the picture exactly. My hair has natural curl, so I can't opt for a straight look. It's easier for me start the day with a little curl and keep it the rest of the day.

And be willing to change with the styles. You may be surprised at how good you look.

2. Ask someone whose hair you like where they have it done.

I'm a firm believer that the best place to find a great hair stylist is from the people around you. Ask your friends, family, co-workers, acquaintances, or even strangers. The key is that you ask people whose hair you'd love to copy.

–Kendra Aarhus

Asking your friends for the name of a good restaurant or a dentist isn't a big deal. So if you admire someone's hairstyle, maybe her hairdresser can make yours look just as good. Feel free to ask anyone you see, friend or not. I once asked a woman on a bus and got connected with a great stylist.

Don't be afraid to ask. I would be flattered if someone wanted to copy my look, so others may be as well.

Sometimes the stylist is out of your price range. That happened to me, since I'm cheap. In that case, remember the style and try to find a similar picture in a magazine or online. Take it to a reasonably-priced stylist and ask him or her to copy it.

3. Observe your stylist so you can do your hair at home.

I think that the most important thing a woman can have—next to talent, of course—is her hairdresser.

–Joan Crawford

Remember those glamour studios in the malls where you could get all dolled up and have your picture taken? My cousin and I had a great time there and we looked terrific that afternoon. But the next day we went back to our usual non-glamorous selves. All we had left was a fabulous picture to remind us how beautiful we once were.

That can happen if we don't pay attention.

When you have your hair cut and styled, talk with your beautician. Ask how they do things and what products they use. Observe how they blow dry, brush, and curl your hair. Then, try it yourself at home. It'll take practice to get results you like, but it will be worth it.

Don't be afraid to attempt something new. Remember, there was a time when you didn't even know how to comb or brush your hair, yet look at what you can do today. Just keep learning and trying, and you can look fabulous every day.

4. Use the correct shampoo.

> *I still get excited in hotel rooms just to see what kind of shampoo they've left me.*
>
> **–Bill Bryson**

When I was young, we used "soap" for shampoo. Our hair was clean, but it could also be dry, frizzy or flaky. Then, we tried dandruff shampoo but I still had dry, frizzy hair.

There are now so many different types and brands of shampoo that it can be overwhelming. Read labels carefully and pick the one best suited for your hair.

First, determine the type of hair you have: dry, oily, normal, permed, or colored. You can discuss this with your hairstylist. Their hands are in your hair more than anyone else's, so they would know.

Next, find the type of shampoo that matches. If more than one word describes your hair, like dry and permed, go with the shampoo for chemically-treated hair, like permed or colored. It will neutralize the dry or oily issue without affecting the color or the curl.

If you're traveling and forgot to pack your shampoo, don't panic. When you have a chance to buy it, do so, but not a large bottle if you're flying. You'd have to leave it behind for security reasons. I still have a large bottle of Axe shampoo in my guest room from my son's visit. He couldn't put the liquid in his carry-on, so there it sits, awaiting his return.

5. Condition every time you shampoo.

Shampoo is better! I go on first and clean the hair! Conditioner is better! I make the hair silky and smooth!
–Billy Madison

After shampooing, oils naturally on the hair shafts are washed away. Your hair can become flyaway and need some taming. That's where conditioner comes in.

Brushing from scalp to hair ends can distribute natural oil and make your hair healthier. But use something to keep it under control while you brush it and while it's drying. That's what conditioners do, as well as adding shine.

Several of my friends had long hair. Without conditioner, there were so many tangles, they couldn't get a comb through it. But when they used a conditioning rinse, those kinks came right out, and they had less breakage.

You may not need to buy the most expensive creams or rinses, but the cheapest probably isn't the best idea either. I used the 99-cent bottles for years until I had a coupon for a "designer" conditioner. As it turns out, I used half as much as my cheaper brand, so it ended up costing less.

The silky feeling you get from conditioning your hair will stick around after you rinse out the excess. If it doesn't, keep shopping until you find the right product.

6. Every other day, skip the shampoo.

> *The hair is the richest ornament of women.*
> **–Martin Luther**

Shampooing every day can be harsh, especially on long hair, which may become over-dry, flyaway or hard to tame. Your hair could also break off or fall out. If any of that happens, skip the shampoo every other day; just rinse your hair and use conditioner. Your hair probably doesn't get very dirty or greasy unless you physically exert yourself. So a rinse could be all you need.

If you work hard in the garden, do housework, or engage in physical activities with sweat dripping, you probably need to shampoo. Go ahead, but rinse out all the soap and apply conditioner. Then, rinse again and have fun styling.

On days that your hair needs less attention, you could apply conditioner just to the ends to keep them from becoming too dry. Two of my friends with very long hair used this tip for years. It saves time, water, and shampoo. And until they told me, I couldn't tell the difference.

I tried it, but my hair doesn't give up "bedhead" and a shampoo to remove the previous day's products. So I still shampoo every day, but you might be able to skip it.

7. Color your hair if you want.

> *The glory of young men is their strength, gray hair the splendor of the old.*
> **–Proverbs 20:29**

My hair is naturally light brown with auburn highlights. At least I think so.

When I was in my thirties, a few gray hairs appeared. I decided to cover the gray with light brown dye. However, it darkened the rest of my hair instead, so the gray was even more obvious. The only way to camouflage the gray hairs was to lighten all the others. So I went blonde.

That worked for several years, until my husband Bryan was watching as I colored my hair. He said, "If you ever want to change the color, I've always wanted to make love to a redhead."

It took a while to get used to my new color, but all the compliments made it easy to decide to keep it. Now, red hair is a part of who I am, and I'll probably stay red until I die or go bald!

Several of my friends embrace their gray hair. You can see some of them on the cover. They wouldn't dream of changing the color, and they look fabulous. But my skin is so light that I look washed out with gray around my face. So I choose to go red.

Dyeing your hair needn't cost a fortune. I buy my brand at a grocery or drug store, wherever it's on sale. And it only takes about a half hour once a month.

If you have a stylist color your hair, be prepared to spend quite a bit, although it might be worth it. They may try to talk you into adding streaks for an additional charge. I know a lady with beautiful blonde hair, who decided that people didn't take her seriously. Now she pays big bucks to have brown streaks added to her hair. She has received respect from her coworkers and advanced in her career. Not sure the brown streaks had much to do with that, but she's convinced.

My ten-year-old twin granddaughters had a streak of color added to their blonde hair—one was hot pink and the other electric blue. They got compliments all the time. I'm thinking about copying it, but that may not look so good in my red hair.

My grandmother and great-aunt used to have "bluing" applied to their gray hair. Sometimes it looked *really* blue. I guess that's why they were called Blue Hairs. Gramma and Aunt liked it, and you may as well.

When you color your hair, you can't tell what the final shade will be by looking at the box. You must complete the coloring process, dry your hair, and then judge for yourself. Be open-minded when you look in the mirror. The first glimpse of the "new you" may be a shock. Give it time.

And get feedback from family and friends, not just your hairdresser. Professionals will likely tell you it looks great. Or that it looks bad so you'll pay to have them fix it.

Color your hair if you want, but don't feel that you have to. It's your choice.

8. Lighten the color as your skin gets lighter.

My hair is not really white; it's kind of grayish, and I don't like the color. So I make it totally white with Klorane dry shampoo. That is the best thing to do because my hair is always clean.

–Karl Lagerfeld

As we age, the pigments in our skin can go berserk. They create age spots in some places, leaving the rest of the skin lighter than before. We may need to adjust some of the temporary coloring for our skin and hair.

Have you ever seen a woman with porcelain skin and jet black hair? I have. She looked like a ghost because of the extreme contrast. And her wrinkles appeared more prominent. Maybe if she had gone a shade or two lighter, she could still have the dramatic look she was after and been fabulous instead of ghostly.

You may need to alter your makeup to match the new color framing your face. Try something new, like darker lipstick or more dramatic eye shadow. You'll be amazed at how fabulous you can look.

9. Don't let your roots tell your secret.

I love to see old women. I love wrinkles. I love gray hair.
–Alber Elbaz

Have you ever seen a skunk on someone's head? That's when she has colored her hair and the roots are growing out, so white or gray shows along her part. Sometimes that's the fashion: color your hair, all but the first half inch or so. If that's the style you're looking for, ignore this suggestion. Otherwise, keep reading.

You'll need to color your hair about once a month. Shorter hair can be dyed less often, especially if you may don't a definite part exposing the roots. A friend of mine has long hair, so she always has it parted. When the roots along the part are gray, she wears a cute hat until she can get an appointment at her salon.

Some beauty companies offer products to touch-up your roots. There are also spray-in colors, applied like hairspray along the part in your hair. These can wash out easily.

One company offers a mascara-type applicator to touch up your roots. It works, but a friend said the liquid spilled onto her scalp and colored it like a permanent marker. To avoid that, hold up a small section of hair and brush from the roots up, reducing the drips. Then, use a cotton swab to blend it into the dyed hair.

You may want streaks to blend in the gray or something totally different. Give it a try, and see how you like it.

10. Have regular haircuts.

Too bad all the people who know how to run this country are busy running taxicabs or cutting hair.
–George Burns

Washing, brushing, and blow-drying can take a toll on your tresses. The ends can become dry and frayed, so when you comb or brush them, you risk breaking them off.

The solution? Even if you're letting your hair grow out, get a trim every month or so. It'll shape your 'do and help you look more put-together. Plus, it's easier on your hair if you don't have flyaway ends to tangle or get caught in your brush and break off.

Here's a creative solution: learn to trim your own hair. It can save the cost of a partial haircut. When my beautician of eight years decided to move to another state, I shopped around for another. I would explain what I was looking for and let them cut. Then, when I got home, I'd get out my scissors and trim my hair to what I really wanted.

After I tried three stylists and recut my hair all three times, I got rid of the middle man and cut my own hair. Since I'd been watching my stylist closely for many years, it wasn't hard.

I'd recommend that you use scissors specifically made for hair, because they're sharper and will give you a cleaner snip. You can buy them at any beauty supply, grocery or drugstore. Even if all you trim is your bangs to give you an extra week between cuts, it'll be worth it. Just be sure the left and right sides of your head match so you don't look lopsided, unless that's the look you're going for.

Whether you do it yourself or trust a professional, having regular cuts is good for both you and your hair.

Your hair is your crowning glory. That doesn't mean that it needs to be big and sparkly like a tiara, but it is the finishing touch on your appearance. Give your tresses the care and attention they need, and you can look and feel fabulous.

Your head crowns you like Mount Carmel.
Your hair is like royal tapestry;
the king is held captive by its tresses.
–Song of Solomon 7:5

Chapter 5

CLOTHING

I never leaf through a copy of National Geographic without realizing how lucky we are to live in a society where it is traditional to wear clothes.

–Erma Bombeck

e've heard that "clothes make the man." Well, clothes make the woman as well. And just a few wardrobe tweaks can make your clothes fabulous. It needn't cost a fortune; just add pizzazz to what you already own.

Growing up, I was the youngest of three girls, so most of what I wore were hand-me-downs. Things didn't fit right and were worn out, but that's what I was given, so that's what I wore. My sister and I shared a bedroom with little closet space, and we didn't have room for a lot of clothes. I wasn't a fashion plate then, but I learned how to accessorize and make the most of what I had.

Today, I have a walk-in closet with lots of clothes, which is both a blessing and a curse. I have many choices of what to wear, which can take more time to get ready in the morning.

Here are some ideas to make the most of the clothes you already have and what to add to make you more fabulous than you can imagine.

1. Wear clothes that fit right.

Diets, like clothes, should be tailored to you.
–Joan Rivers

Do you know your size? Maybe you do, and it's probably not the size you want to wear. Most women are unhappy with their dress size, some because it's a higher number than they'd like, and some because it's lower.

I know a lady who was Size 4 on her wedding day. Within the next few years, she had three children and her body changed, which is normal. Unfortunately, she couldn't admit to herself that she now wore a larger size. She still bought clothes in Size 4, although she bulged out, created a "muffin top," and popped buttons. Once someone convinced her to try on clothes in the correct size, she again looked fabulous and didn't have to squeeze into a Size 4 to do it.

When shopping for a wedding gown on my lunch hour (true story), a friend was with me. I got weepy when one size didn't fit. My friend, who was very thin, told me, "Size is just a number. It doesn't mean anything."

"But it's a higher number than I wish it was," I said.

"That doesn't matter. What matters is that we get the dress that fits you best and looks absolutely fabulous on you. A smaller size won't do that."

So that's what we did. I bought a larger size, and no one else knew what size it was, so it didn't matter. And I looked fabulous, if I do say so.

Did you know that high-end designers cut their clothing larger than the clothes most of us wear? An expensive Size 4 and a cheaper Size 10 can be identical in dimensions, but I think rich women would rather say they wear a Size 4. The same is true of gift shops in resort areas. They want tourists to be enticed into buying their clothing, so the garments are labeled as smaller sizes.

The trick is to wear clothing that fits you, whatever the size.

I tried wearing my smaller clothes. I couldn't believe the bulges that weren't there the last time I wore those slacks. And the waistband choked off my digestive system. Unfortunately, I popped a few buttons, too.

And I tried the bigger-is-better route, where you buy a size or two larger than you should, hoping that the bagginess makes you look thinner. Unfortunately, it only made me appear large and frumpy and encouraged me to eat until I filled up the bigger clothes.

When I finally admitted what size I was and wore garments in that size, I looked more natural and felt relaxed. Instead of constantly holding in my stomach or tugging at my blouse, I was confident in my appearance and comfortable in my own body.

You can get the same results. Figure out what size your body is. The number isn't important, especially since there is no standard sizing. Then wear only clothes that fit. You'll feel more at ease, have more confidence and be fabulous.

2. Use a full-length mirror.

I sometimes stand in front of a mirror and change a million times because I know I really want to wear my nightgown.
–Gilda Radner

I always thought a full-length mirror was for women with dressing tables and satin robes, not me. I just looked in the mirror over the bathroom sink and let it go at that.

Then came the day when every time I turned around, my slip was hanging below my hemline. And friends and co-workers were only too happy to point it out.

I realized that the mirror over the sink only showed one-fourth of my appearance. The top front looked good, but what about the bottom front and the top and bottom of the back?

That's when I decided to get a full-length mirror. The first one cost about five dollars and hung on the closet door. It was exactly what I needed—a way to get the entire picture. I learned that some shoes worked better with my slacks than others and some hemlines were crooked.

When I moved to a house with a large bathroom, I purchased a cheval mirror, the kind on a stand that swivels so you can adjust it to your eye height. I can now see exactly how I look and feel better when I go out in public. You can find these mirrors for around $30. It's worth the investment if you have the room.

3. Try on all your clothes.

I'm a bit of a clothes hoarder, admittedly.
–Jennifer Aniston

This is a fun exercise! Take a Saturday afternoon, a couple of hours or so, and try on every article of clothing in your closet and your dresser. I'm serious—try everything on, even socks you haven't worn in years. You may be surprised at what looks good and what doesn't.

With each piece, ask three questions:

1. *Does this fit me?*

   Does it really fit your body as it is today, not what you hope it will be when you lose a few pounds? Maybe you found a fabulous dress that was a little too small. You planned to wear it when your diet finally worked. But that dress has never been worn, so get rid of it.

2. *Is it in good shape?*

   Could you walk out the door right now? Maybe it has a grease spot, a missing button, or a loose hem, something that could be mended quickly. If so, fix it and wear it. But if it's not worth repairing, no sense holding onto it.

   One note about grease spots: My favorite laundry product is Dawn® dishwashing detergent. One of its taglines is, "Dawn cuts through grease." So I squirt it on those spots and relaunder, even after the article has already been through the dryer. I've used it on cotton, rayon, linen, and a Colorado Avalanche sports jersey. It worked every time.

3. *How do I feel in it?*

   If that piece of clothing makes you feel confident or beautiful, by all means keep it and enjoy it. But if you tug it to make it fit better or you're not quite sure, it probably isn't right for you. Pass it on to someone else or throw it away.

I can't tell you how freeing this was for me. I had some "skinny clothes" hanging in my closet reminding me every day that I had added pounds. When I lost weight, there were some articles too big that I would never alter to my new shape. So I got rid of a lot of things, including some that I didn't like and probably wouldn't wear again.

That gave me more closet space so the clothes left were no longer squished together, pressing wrinkles into them. And it was easier to find something, since I had fewer clothes to slide back and forth.

When done with the closet, tackle your dresser drawers. No sense wasting space, even if it's something hideous your mother-in-law gave you for your birthday. This might be the perfect excuse to get rid of it. Worked for me!

4. Get rid of clothes you won't wear.

The expression a woman wears on her face is far more important than the clothes she wears on her back.
–Dale Carnegie

If you have friends who have no problems wearing hand-me-overs, offer them your extras, especially if they've hinted that they'd like them. I wouldn't insult anyone by offering them garments I was going to throw out, but most of my clothes are in pretty good shape when I'm done with them.

One friend is about my size, as are her daughters. So when I'm done with some clothes, I offer them to her, and what they don't wear is donated.

I have no issue wearing previously-owned garments, as long as they look fabulous. In fact, most of my clothes are from thrift stores, fashionably called "vintage."

Charities can always use donations. Keep a large plastic bag in your closet. When you decide you don't want something any more, put it in the bag right away so you won't be tempted to hang it back up.

(Frugal Franny coming out here.) If you sew and you're throwing away a garment, remove buttons, zippers, or other notions first. I've even bought things at thrift stores just because I liked the buttons or decorations and wanted to use them on something else. No sense getting rid of the notions because you don't like the entire article.

5. Organize your closet.

If I don't do laundry today, I'm gonna have to buy new clothes tomorrow.

–Anna Paquin

Once you get rid of some things, organize what's left to make it easier to find the clothes you're looking for. I used to spend too much time thumbing through the closet, shoving hangers back and forth, looking for a particular blouse or skirt. Now, I hang like garments together: dresses, suits, jackets, tops/blouses, skirts, and slacks. That narrows down the space and time needed to find something.

In order to expand your closet capacity, get some multiple clothes hangers, also known as cascading hangers. They hang from the clothes rod and have several holes or slots to insert hangers, so you can put five or six items in the space normally taken up by one hanger.

Sort all items by color, so if your fuchsia turtleneck is in the laundry, your other pink tops are nearby to choose from. I've even put long-sleeved or short-sleeved blouses together, again by color. It saves lots of time, and I find more options when I'm looking for a particular item.

Here's a way to purge your closet annually: Hang all your clothes so the front of each garment is facing to the right. As you wear and launder an article, hang it so the front is facing to the left. After one year, you can easily see what you haven't worn. Every item facing to the right hasn't been touched, so you can probably get rid of it. Since everything is now facing left, as you wear and launder items, hang them facing right. At the end of the next year, get rid of the clothes still facing left.

After I taught this in a workshop, one attendee contacted me. She had followed this suggestion and reduced the amount of time it took for her to get ready every morning. She said excitedly, "I never dreamed that just arranging things in my closet would make me feel so good."

6. Become more feminine from the skin out.

She had a womanly instinct that clothes possess an influence more powerful over many than the worth of character or the magic of manners.

–Louisa May Alcott

When I was younger, my mom told me, "Good girls wear only white cotton bras and panties." I followed those instructions, which wasn't exactly a turn-on for my husband.

My life and attitude improved when I changed to lacy bras and panties. This story is in Chapter 1, Section 1, #1. "You don't have to be as old as you used to be."

After hearing this suggestion, one friend reluctantly tried lacy underwear, then confided that it really did make a difference for her. She felt pretty and more like a woman, not just a mom. In fact, she felt so good that she went back and bought more, so she could have that feeling every day.

Find a bra style that works for you and is comfortable enough to wear from dawn till bedtime. You can go to a "foundations" store or a lingerie department to have an expert fit you. Then, buy other bras at your regular store.

A saleslady once suggested that I wear a lightly-padded bra. I laughed and told her I didn't need the extra size. She explained that padding was more for support than for shaping. And she was right. I tried one and felt more comfortable than I had been in years.

Another thing I tried was underwire bras. That extra bit of support helped to shape my breasts from normal-hanging triangles into circles, which I prefer. Underwire bras work great for me, but several of my friends were horrified at the thought. Some ladies were small-chested and didn't need the support; others said the wires poked more than they helped. Try one to see which you prefer.

Since I didn't have a lot of extra cash to replace everything, I changed a few pieces at a time. I started at lingerie-only stores. That's where I learned my correct size and made a few small purchases from the sale racks.

But I didn't always go to lingerie stores to find what I was looking for. Department and discount stores had feminine undergarments at reasonable prices. Unfortunately, the bigger your "girls" are, the more you'll have to spend for the support you need.

I have black, hot pink, and purple panties and bras to wear with certain outfits. But most of my undergarments are flesh-colored for good reason. At the end of one vacation, the only clean shorts left were white, and my only clean pair of panties had red and white stripes. Each might have looked great, but not together: the stripes showed through the shorts.

So now I make sure to wear underwear that isn't visible under my clothes.

7. Buy quality clothes.

Humility and knowledge in poor clothes excel pride and ignorance in costly attire.

–William Penn

When my stepchildren were teens, they received a clothing budget each fall to spend as they wanted for school. Lisa would hit thrift stores and discount stores. She purchased dozens of articles of clothing and created a lot of outfits. Her brother would buy only clothes with designer labels, just a few items for that school year. He combined these with previous years' purchases to make several looks. Each was happy with his or her choice.

The downside with Lisa's approach was that her trendy clothes were not as well-made and didn't last as long. But she could buy what was in fashion and replace it the next year. Her brother's clothes were classic styles that could endure many seasons, but there were fewer to choose from. That's not a big deal for a guy, but might be an issue for a woman.

Most of us want options, so we don't have to resort to, "I don't have anything to wear!" Instead, consider buying classic styles that don't go out of fashion.

8. Find great clothes at a thrift store.

Expensive clothes are a waste of money.
–Meryl Streep

A garment is only new once; after you've worn it, it's used. You probably clean it before wearing it again. Same for used clothing. You'll wash or dry clean it before you wear it, so what's the difference whether the person who wore it last was you or someone else?

Some people have a problem just entering a thrift store, let alone wearing something bought there. Not me. Growing up in a poor family, I regularly wore clothes that were not new.

To me, it's like buying a used car instead of new. That new car depreciates so much when you drive it off the lot, it's probably not worth it. It's instantly a used car and worth much less.

I could never afford designer Liz Claiborne, Jones New York, and Gloria Vanderbilt clothing new. But I have some of each, most priced less than five dollars at thrift stores.

Think of it as going green in your closet. Instead of throwing old clothes away and buying a new wardrobe, you're recycling and reducing landfill. And your old clothes can be recycled into some else's closet.

Here's a tip: shop at resale stores or garage sales in neighborhoods where you would like to live. Since many donations are made onsite, garments are usually things the neighbors don't want any longer. If you're comfortable with that, shop there. Otherwise, go to a neighborhood similar to yours or one step up the economic ladder.

Consignment stores offer pre-owned clothing, usually a higher quality than thrift stores. Prices are higher as well, but may be worth it. I was looking for a long-sleeved red blouse for a Christmas show at church and went to several thrift stores with no luck. At a consignment store, I found a beautiful red silk blouse for $12.00. The original tags indicated a price of $104.00, for a savings of $92.00. Shopping around was worth the time and effort.

9. Wear clothing for your body type.

I love clothes, but I don't know what to put on myself, let alone others. I have a lot of help getting dressed.
–Jennifer Aniston

Have you ever tried on a new fashion, only to discover that it looks horrible on you? Maybe your chest is too large/small, your hips too curvy/straight, or you fill it out in the wrong spot. The worst is "One Size Fits None." No matter what size or shape you are, it won't fit.

That has happened to me often, starting in high school when "shrink tops" were in style. Those were crocheted yarn granny squares assembled into a rectangular pullover vest that looked great if you had a boyish body like Twiggy. Unfortunately, the little rascals didn't fit over my bosom, so I was out of fashion for several years.

Now that we've matured, we don't need to follow trends. We can create our own look based on our body type and clothes we already have. No matter what shape you are, you can look fabulous. Just be honest about what looks best on you.

A few ideas to consider for your wardrobe:

- Monochromatic (one color top to bottom) can make you look slimmer and taller.
- Vertical stripes give the illusion of height, except with tight-fitting knits. These tend to follow curves and accentuate bulges.
- Begin with basic neutrals (white, beige, navy blue, black) and add splashes of color with a jacket, scarf, or jewelry.
- A jacket draws the eye to its hem, so a shorter jacket can actually make your hips appear smaller.
- Full or pleated skirts add width from the waist down.
- Take a friend shopping with you. She can tell you what looks fabulous and what doesn't.

Be objective when you look in a mirror, whether in a fitting room or at home. Notice how the clothes hang, whether the hem is straight or not, and if the length is right for the shoes you're wearing.

Don't put anything in your closet that you don't absolutely love.

10. Accessorize to add fabulosity.

I love being a woman and I was not one of these women who rose through professional life by wearing men's clothes and looking masculine. I loved wearing bright colors and being who I am.
–Madeline Albright

An accessory is something worn for a fashion effect and can be anything from jewelry to scarves, hats and gloves. You don't need a lot, but you do need something to complement your outfit. Otherwise, you're just a three-dimensional hanger.

Jewelry can add a touch of class and color.

There was a time when I wore only tiny earrings and a thin chain necklace with a small heart. Very boring and not fabulous at all. Today, I go for color in my jewelry, often buying a set so all the elements match. Nothing expensive, just costume jewelry, but gorgeous nonetheless.

Start with a necklace or a scarf. It can be the same shade as the top you're wearing or a complementary color. Or pick up an accent color from the rest of your outfit. Either way, you'll look put-together.

Add other accessories, like earrings or a pin or a flower on your lapel. Keep adding until you feel really good about the way you look. Check the mirror, and when you're smiling, you're *almost* done.

Now, take one thing off. That's right, take one thing off. For some reason, when you remove one accessory, no matter which one, you'll be amazed at how much better you look.

> *I personally battled with my own body image for years. I used to tell myself, "You can't wear anything sleeveless or strapless." And all of a sudden I was like, "What if I just didn't send such negative messages to my brain and said, 'Wear it and enjoy it'?" And now I'm more comfortable in clothes than ever.*
>
> **–Drew Barrymore**

Now, go out and show the world how absolutely fabulous you look, because you do! Remember, fabulous is in the details.

> *Some people, no matter how old they get, never lose their beauty— they merely move it from their faces into their hearts.*
>
> **–Martin Buxbaum**

Section 3

BELIEFS

One life is all we have and we live it as we believe in living it. But to sacrifice what you are and to live without belief, that is a fate more terrible than dying.

–Joan of Arc

Raised in a Christian home, I was at church every time the doors were open. "Thou shalt" and "Thou shalt not" were the law in our house. I was a submissive child who did, said, and believed as I was told. But when I was a teen, I questioned Christianity. There were a few useless issues that I couldn't figure out, so I chucked everything. (What I questioned is not important, but the results are.)

For a while, I was not nice to be around. Everything I had believed was gone and I was floundering. Anger became my close friend, which I didn't like.

After about a month, I sorted out the answers and "nice" Debbie returned. Not only was I more pleasant, but I also owned my beliefs. I had searched for the "why" of Christianity and figured out how it all fit together. Those beliefs became a part of who I am.

It's like breathing. When someone has a respiratory ailment, they concentrate on every breath to be sure they get enough air. Once the problem is controlled, inhaling becomes second nature. They don't have to tell their lungs to breathe; it just happens. It is now a part of them and feels natural.

Have you ever thought about what you really believe? Not just what you give lip service to, but what you really, deep-down, totally-convinced-of believe.

As Jon Stewart puts it, "If you don't stick to your values when they're being tested, they're not values; they're hobbies." You can do a hobby for a few minutes here and there, but it won't have much impact on your life. A belief lives with you 24/7.

When my husband Bryan was dying of cancer, I had to determine if I really believed in Christianity or if it was just something for Sunday mornings. If there was any hope for Bryan or a chance to see him after death, it all had to be true.

My faith helped me through those dark hours as I watched him pass into eternity and learned to live without him. I have no idea how someone can lose a loved one without hope of ever seeing them again.

Let's look at how our beliefs can become a fabulous part of who we are.

Chapter 6

ATTITUDE

Attitude is more important than the past, than education, than money, than circumstances, than what people do or say. It is more important than appearance, giftedness, or skill.
–Charles R. Swindoll

Since I had been abused and lived in the projects as a child, I felt I deserved a better adulthood. Never mind that others had a worse home life. I still wanted special treatment, especially from my husband and family. When they didn't come through, I let them know—frequently.

I remained a victim for years, complaining to anyone who would listen. When something didn't go my way, I became vocal. My car horn got a workout every time someone changed lanes or made me slow down.

Note Chuck Swindoll's quote above. Listening to him speak about attitude helped me to improve mine. And changing my attitude made all the difference.

When I wake in the morning now, I decide to have a good day. And that's usually what happens. Even when my car was rear-ended or my husband received his cancer diagnosis, it wasn't devastating. That positive attitude helped my mind to stay clear and not wallow in the depths of despair.

Here are some ways you can control your attitude.

1. Choose joy.

People are like stained-glass windows. They sparkle and shine when the sun is out, but when the darkness sets in, their true beauty is revealed only if there is a light from within.
–Elisabeth Kubler-Ross

Bad things happen to everybody.

I once decided to write a book about all the rotten things I've overcome. My outline had one misfortune in each chapter. When I reached twenty-five chapters, I opted not to write the book. Nobody needs to read all that garbage.

Those things I've lived through are why I'm known as the Queen of Resilience. I've learned how to overcome bad things and not remain a victim.

Some folks enjoy being a victim, complaining and telling everyone what happened to them. They may not realize that their response to life is up to them.

Maybe your first reaction to something tragic would be to yell, cry, lash out, or withdraw. All of those responses are normal. It's also the first step in dealing with experiences. But your ultimate response is a choice.

I've had a variety of reactions to different catastrophes. When Mom died, I wanted to be alone and cry. Years later, when my husband nearly died after a serious car accident, I became angry and threw things. When my son got in trouble with the law, all I could do was moan and sob. I had trouble functioning normally or even praying.

Maybe you've gone through or are dealing with something right now and reacting in your own way. That's fine, as long as you don't hurt yourself or anyone else.

After the initial shock, your brain re-engages and you look at things more objectively. That's when to choose your response. You could continue in a fog and not resume normal activities or you can re-enter life.

It may feel wrong to choose joy when you've lost a loved one. But once you know what joy is and isn't, it's easier to opt for that.

Joy is not happiness. Nor is it ignorant glee or fake cheerfulness.

On "Adventures in Odyssey," a kids' radio program by Focus on the Family, I heard a great definition: "Happiness is a response to a set of circumstances, but joy is a smile deep down inside of you." That means you can smile on the inside even when your outside can't.

Responses to tragedy are similar to dealing with death, so let me just mention the stages of grief, as outlined by Elizabeth Kubler Ross in her book, "On Death and Dying." [2] They are:

1. Denial—this can't be happening
2. Anger—we lash out at anyone and anything
3. Bargaining—if only … I wish … God, if you'll …
4. Depression—which may need some help to conquer
5. Acceptance—moving on with your life

You don't always go from Stage 1 through Stage 5 in that order. Most journeys through grief involve bouncing around, slipping backward and forward, maybe dealing with more than one step at a time.

Too often, people never move from one of the first four steps, which isn't healthy for them or anyone around them.

When my husband died, I was devastated, even though we knew for months that his cancer was terminal. I yelled at God, cried, and paced my house for hours on end. The world seemed gray, cloudier than normal. After a year of sliding through the stages of grief, I finally realized that I had a choice—continue this way and remain an angry, bitter woman, or allow myself to feel joy again.

I chose joy.

It was a major attitude shift. God knew when Bryan would die and had the option of bringing him into my life for a short time or not letting me meet him at all. I was grateful for the opportunity to have Bryan for a few years and focused on that, so joy took up residence. I didn't always feel like smiling on the outside, but the deep-down smile was there and showed itself every once in a while.

You can do it too. Choose to let yourself feel joy and contentment in spite of circumstances.

2. Show your positive attitude.

Your success and happiness lie in you. Resolve to be happy, and your joy and you shall form an invincible host against difficulties.

–Helen Keller

The old adage says, "Fake it till you make it." If you don't really feel happy, paste on a pleasant face until you do. Or pretend that you've already worked through all your negative feelings and smile anyway. The positive feelings will follow.

Some days you may wake up and not feel like doing anything. In fact, you'd rather just stay in bed. You don't feel sick, but when you look in the mirror, you're less than excited about what you see.

That's the time to kick the positive attitude in gear.

Start by smiling at yourself in a mirror. That alone will improve your attitude. It also raises your cheeks and makes your eyes twinkle. A forced smile can eventually become genuine.

The smile is the "fake it" part. Now, do the "make it" part—think positively. Not "I'm positive I'll have a rotten day" or "I'm sure sick." Instead, say, "I look good and feel good. It's going to be a great day."

Ever have one of *those* days, when you spill your coffee in the kitchen, then drop a raw egg on the floor? I did—recently. If you tell yourself, "Well, I'm gonna be clumsy today," your brain sends that message to your body, and you end up being a klutz. Not a good day.

Here's an alternative: after cleaning up the coffee and the egg, tell yourself, "Glad I got that out of the way. Now it'll be a terrific day." And you know what? It just might! Your brain will tell your body and the day can turn around, much to your surprise.

This is not a Pollyanna approach, head in the clouds, oblivious to reality. Don't pretend that life is perfect. That won't solve your problems. Instead, decide to respond positively to whatever happens, good or bad. You could improve your day as a result.

Here are some examples of famous people who remained positive in spite of circumstances:

- **Sonya Carson**, mother of Dr. Ben Carson, the subject of the book and movie, "Gifted Hands: The Ben Carson Story," worked three jobs as a single mom. Despite financial problems and a bigamist husband, she continually told Ben he could do whatever he wanted. Ben is the first surgeon to successfully separate twins conjoined at the head and has gone on to receive the Presidential Medal of Freedom. He credits his mother's attitude and belief in him as major reasons for his success.[3]

- **Elizabeth Edwards** was married to John Edwards, whose indiscretions came to light while he was running for US Vice President. Elizabeth was later diagnosed with terminal cancer. In spite of it all, she said, "A positive attitude is not going to save you. What it's going to do is, every day, between now and the day you die, whether that's a short time from now or a long time from now, that every day, you're going to actually live."[4]

- According to television host **Joan Lunden**, "A positive attitude is something everyone can work on, and everyone can learn how to employ it."[5] Her attitude propelled her to co-anchor Good Morning America shortly after joining the show as a feature news reporter.[6] She was so popular with viewers that GMA lost about four million viewers when she left the show.[7]

- One of my favorite statements about positive attitudes comes from **Chuck Swindoll**: "I believe the single most significant decision I can make on a day-to-day basis is my choice of attitude. It is more important than my past, my education, my bankroll, my successes or failures, fame or pain, what other people think of me or say about me, my circumstances, or my position. Attitude keeps me going or cripples my progress. It alone fuels my fire or assaults my hope. When my attitudes are right, there is no barrier too high, no valley too deep, no dream too extreme, no challenge too great for me."[8]

I can't promise that you won't ever have a bad day. But the difference between failure and success is getting up one more time.

3. Develop a sense of humor.

A person without a sense of humor is like a wagon without springs. It's jolted by every pebble on the road.

–Henry Ward Beecher

This is my absolute very favorite subject in the whole world—humor.

Laughter can break down barriers, cement friendships, mend broken relationships, and soothe ruffled feathers. It is also a great ice-breaker for speakers and their audiences. People remember what they laugh about, more than what they hear or see.

Laughter is the shortest distance between two people.
–Victor Borge

Laughing is fun, relaxing, and good for your health. Studies have shown that having a good laugh every day can lead to emotional well-being. It may also help your body resist disease for several days.[9]

Humor is a great way to color not-so-good experiences. Maybe things went wrong and someone said, "One day we'll laugh about this." Later, tell the story and laugh.

Here's one of my laugh-later tales: Bryan and I decided to take advantage of a Buy-One-Get-One-Free coupon at a restaurant 40 miles away. The fact that there were only two cars in the parking lot should've told us to drive on by, but we decided this would be "an adventure."

Upon entering, instead of being tantalized by the aroma of barbecue, we were overcome with the smell of pine cleaner. The dinner was passable, not bad for what we paid, but too much food. When we asked the oversized, under-shaven waiter for to-go boxes, he handed us each a sheet of aluminum foil. We took home BBQ pork, baked beans, and cole slaw wrapped in foil. What a mess!

We laughed over that for years, which was much better than complaining or getting upset. Humor made the experience cement our relationship instead of creating a rift.

Laughter can also help in serious times. After Mom died, my siblings and I gathered at my sister's house, where we ate, slept, and reminisced. We'd sit around and talk about Mom, starting with, "Do you remember the time…?" and then we'd laugh at the memories. It helped us work through our grief.

> *Mirth is God's medicine. Everybody ought to bathe in it.*
> **–Henry Ward Beecher**

Let's jump in. The water's great!

4. Stay away from negative attitudes, yours and others'.

> *Our attitude towards others determines their attitude towards us.*
> **–Earl Nightingale**

Have you ever been around someone with such a negative view that they drag you down? I worked with someone like that once. Office morale was in the toilet, so it was difficult to be content with my job. "Laura" approached my desk and started complaining.

I turned to her and said, "Laura, I have a hard enough time keeping a positive attitude in this place. I don't need you to add to the problem."

"Well!" she snorted. "I guess I just won't talk to you anymore." And with that, she turned and stomped away.

I breathed a quiet, "Thank you. That's exactly what I wanted." During the three weeks that she stayed away from me, my morale improved dramatically!

Just because you're stuck with someone, whether at work, in a Bible study, or in your own family, doesn't mean they get to determine your attitude. Everyone has problems, but they needn't dump them on you.

Set boundaries and limit the time you spend with them. If they overstep your boundary, excuse yourself and leave. When they ask, tell them politely that you have trouble maintaining a positive attitude, and you need to go work on it.

I know this seems trite, but it's one way to protect yourself. As Dr. Phil McGraw frequently says, "You teach people how to treat you."[10] If you say nothing and just take it, you're telling them they can continue to be negative.

By speaking up and leaving when they start griping, you teach them that you won't tolerate it. High blood pressure is a great excuse, so tell them your doctor told you to get out of stressful situations, and they're creating one.

Maintaining a positive attitude is a daily, moment-by-moment choice. You alone are responsible for your attitude, and that's one thing you control all the time. If you have folks around you who share your positive outlook, life is much easier.

5. Forgive another who has controlled your life for too long.

I'm going to stand before God and give an account of my life, not for somebody else's life. If I have a bad attitude, then I need to say there's no point in me blaming you for what's wrong in my life.
–Joyce Meyer

Forgiveness is a difficult issue to face.

Many people have the mistaken impression that the phrase "forgive and forget" means you need to do exactly that: let the other person off the hook and release them with no consequences or revenge and forget what happened.

Not true. Forgiveness is *all about you* and *not about them.*

When I was preparing to marry Bryan, he delivered an ultimatum one month before the ceremony. He told me that whenever I talked about my abusive father, my eyes would blaze and "green smoke" would come out of my mouth. He said I had to let go of the past and forgive my father or there would be no wedding. Bryan would not allow that hatred to poison our marriage.

I replied, "If I haven't forgiven him in 35 years, how can I forgive him in 30 days?"

"Not my problem," he said.

I was so mad, I almost took off my engagement ring and threw it at him. Fortunately, I decided to try forgiveness, or at least make it look like I tried.

Since I didn't understand how to forgive, I figured I'd read a book, tell Bryan I had met his ultimatum, and then take time after the wedding to actually work on forgiving my dad. My local bookstore carried "The Freedom of Forgiveness" by David Augsberger, which explained the process beautifully. This book made the difference for me.

Here's the secret: Forgiveness is a shift in your attitude. Whatever happened in the past will no longer control you. It may sound simplistic, but that's what forgiveness is. I only had to read half the book to finally understand what forgiveness is and let go of what had been controlling me for years.

That night, Bryan came to pick me up for dinner, took one look at me, and said, "You forgave your father, didn't you?" He said it showed on my face: my features were more relaxed, my eyes were clearer, and I appeared happier than he had ever seen me.

I now teach a powerful workshop on forgiveness. Here are my 10 steps to forgiving anyone:

1. Realize that your hate doesn't affect the offender. You're the only one fuming about it.
2. Understand that the best revenge is to live a successful and happy life and to turn what happened into something positive.
3. Make a list of the good that has come as a result, even if it's just assisting someone in a similar circumstance.
4. Look for helpers in the situation. It may have been worse if these folks hadn't been around.

5. Be compassionate with yourself. You don't deserve the pain and guilt you inflict on yourself.

6. Balance trust with wisdom. Forgiving an abuser doesn't mean giving them the chance to hurt you again.

7. Stop telling your story. Rehashing it maintains your status as a victim, and you want to move past it.

8. Look at "the story" from the other person's point of view. Maybe they had a reason for what they did. My dad was abused as a child and couldn't let that go.

9. Maintain perspective. A child, friend, or family member of the offender is not guilty by association, so they don't need to be punished.

10. Decide to take back your life. That person controlled your life far too long. Don't let it continue.

Forgiveness is simple but not easy. It may be the hardest work you've ever done, but I promise it will be worth it.

6. Spend time with those you want to be like.

I've been lucky enough that I can gather all sorts of experiences and find inspiration by traveling around and by spending time with people I admire.

–Bonnie Raitt

When we were younger, our parents told us not to hang out with "the wrong kind" of friends. Maybe they tried to keep you away from kids who were a bad influence. They knew that we'd become like those we spent time with.

The same is true for us as adults, but we need to decide if our friends are good or not. How do we do that? By using railroad-crossing directions: STOP, LOOK, and LISTEN.

I was once involved in a relationship before I took the time to really get to know him and his family. The relationship just kept moving forward and I didn't bother to STOP it when I should have, even when there were red flags.

LOOK objectively at whomever we're spending time with. Maybe we're in awe, excited to be with them, or desperate for a relationship. For me, I loved having someone to cuddle with on the couch, to tell me I'm special, and to have fun with. It's hard to remove rose-colored glasses, so list that person's good qualities and bad habits. It might be difficult to be objective and come up with negatives, so ask for help.

Friends and family can tell what they think of whoever we're spending time with, but we need to LISTEN. During the engagement to my first husband, my sister told me that he appeared to be gay. I laughed it off and said he was just an actor and having fun. Twenty years and two sons later, he came out of the closet. I wish I had listened and prevented all the heartache.

Sometimes, people use one another instead of getting to really know them. Maybe you befriend a car dealer when you're in the market for a new car. Writers may cultivate a friendship with an agent or an editor in the hopes of getting published. Spending time with someone to use them is not a good basis for a relationship.

When I was a young adult, an attractive young man came to church and got to know me and my friends. Turns out, he was a salesman for expensive cooking pans. After he had pitched to every girl in the group, he moved on.

A positive attitude can help you be successful in many areas of your life, so find someone you want to be around, not just someone who can help your career. You just may discover that others want to be around you, so they can acquire your positive attitude.

7. Decide not to allow anger to take over.

Adopting the right attitude can convert a negative stress into a positive one.

–Hans Selye

The first stage of grief is anger. It's okay to be angry; some things will really get to you and invoke a negative reaction.

God expects us to get angry. Ephesians 4:26 says, "In your anger do not sin." We shouldn't let our anger spill out and end up on tonight's news. That's not something we want for ourselves or anyone we know.

But "do not sin" involves something less newsworthy. Seething anger can put a rift in a family or end a friendship. It can also make us gossip or snub someone, possibly even divide a church congregation.

My husband's family was torn apart when one family member was unintentionally offended, became angry, and held onto that grudge for years. Bryan died without that relationship being restored, even though he apologized repeatedly.

Anger might be appropriate, but that's not where God wants us to live. Make a conscious effort to get past the anger, treat the situation like a death and move through the stages of grief. These are listed in Chapter 6, Attitude, 1. "Choose Joy." It might help to review them now. Go ahead. I'll wait...

Try to think "What if?" and change the circumstance. Or go to the person who made you angry and tell them.

Remember, you are not responsible for anyone else's anger. They choose to live with it, and you can't change their minds or their lives. They also must live with their anger's consequences. Just stay out of the range of fire when they take aim.

Living in anger is a choice. When you decide to move to a different "neighborhood," you'll be much happier. Let go and move forward.

8. Control the 90% that's yours.

Life is 10% what happens to you and 90% how you react to it.
–Chuck Swindoll

It took me a while to believe that quote. My dad was abused as a child, and thought that gave him the right to do the same to his wife and all six of his children. For years, I let what happened to me determine my destiny.

Mom did nothing to stop the abuse. She was as afraid of Dad as we were. At one point, I asked her why we didn't leave. "Where would we go?" she replied. "I don't know anybody who would take in a woman with six children. We have to stay here and take it."

So we did. I learned that my older sister had run away years earlier and wouldn't return unless Dad promised to leave her alone. He agreed, but redirected his attention and abuse to the rest of us.

My *response* to the abuse controlled my life, not the fact that it occurred. I could remain a victim, complaining about what someone did and use it as an excuse for not accomplishing anything. Or I could acknowledge it happened, let it go, and take my life back.

We all write our own story, and what happened in the past is only one chapter. Take time to look at your life and decide to take back control of your life, attitude, and future.

9. Reframe your thinking.

When you pray for anyone, you tend to modify your personal attitude toward him.
–Norman Vincent Peale

Most paintings at an art museum have ornate frames to make them look their best. When they were painted, that artwork had no frame. They were ideas translated onto canvas or other material, with only the edges to define the boundaries.

An unframed painting may look plain. But take that painting and put it in a wide frame, maybe with a mat to set off the colors, and you have a striking work of art. The painting hasn't changed at all, but it looks fabulous.

Reframing can help with your memories. Left the way you remember, they're raw and sometimes ugly. Try thinking of those experiences in a different way.

Instead of remembering bad experiences or poor choices you made, choose to view them differently. No longer the nightmare your brain remembers, it is now your version of Oliver Twist, where you might have started as a helpless child but ended up living in a mansion. Picture yourself in that large house, happy and secure. This may take some doing, and a lot of daydreaming, but it can definitely be worth the effort.

Just as your mind focused on bad, it can now focus on good. Those memories can be embedded in luxury instead of the actual circumstances.

Another way to reframe is to see where God was in the event. Some people look back at their lives and ask, "Where was God in all of this? Why didn't he rescue me?"

In Matthew 10, Jesus sends his disciples out and tells them how he would help them. "Are not two sparrows sold for a penny? Yet not one of them will fall to the ground outside your Father's care. So don't be afraid; you are worth more than many sparrows." He doesn't promise that sparrows won't fall, but he cares when they hurt, just as he cares when we hurt.

Although God didn't stop pain in my life, he was with me every moment. He knew what I would face and never gave up on my ability to handle it and that I could help others with their pain. I would have preferred not to endure it all, but I can see God's hand in it.

No matter how bad your memories are, think how much worse it might have been without God. You may be surprised at how you remember differently.

10. Don't think that you can't change.

Develop an attitude of gratitude, and give thanks for everything that happens to you, knowing that every step forward is a step toward achieving something bigger and better than your current situation.

–Brian Tracy

Some things you're born with and can't change, like DNA, ancestors, and facts of your birth. We could also include your height and your family's predisposition to certain diseases or medical conditions.

But being one way doesn't mean you'll stay there your entire life. I don't know any 50-year-old who still weighs 8 pounds, 4 ounces. And everyone I know eventually had teeth and hair, maybe temporarily, since they're in the process of losing both.

Okay, those are obvious things that change. But what about attitudes, thoughts, dreams, even hygiene? We can control and change those whenever we want.

Sometimes negative people don't realize how much they change. Before they left home today, skin was washed, hair combed, teeth brushed, and clothes donned. After going to that much trouble to change their outward appearance, why wouldn't they improve the inside?

Just as we learned to take care of ourselves physically, we can learn to change other things. With practice, we can live a positive life and make ourselves the best we can be. Why cheat ourselves out of that?

Nothing can stop the man with the right mental attitude from achieving his goal; nothing on earth can help the man with the wrong mental attitude.

–Thomas Jefferson

Chapter 7

FAITH

Now faith is confidence in what we hope for
and assurance of what we do not see.
–Hebrews 11:1

aith is not only believing in something, but also expecting a certain outcome and acting on that belief.

When we enter a dark room, we have faith that the switch on the wall will turn on the lights. But just believing doesn't make the lights work. We have to reach out and flip the switch. That's true faith— knowing something, trusting it, and acting on it.

Some people think that those with a religious or spiritual faith act like ostriches, heads in the sand, oblivious to reality. Quite the contrary. Someone with faith is aware of the situation, but choosing to concentrate on the solution instead of the obstacles ahead.

Writing is my personal act of faith. Sitting in my living room, I have ideas and type them into my laptop. There's no guarantee that someone will publish what I write or read those words and act on them, but I write them anyway.

What do you have faith in?

And don't say you don't need faith. You act on faith every time you sit in a chair, get into a car, or send an email. You believe that the chair will hold you, the car will run, and the message will get to the addressee. That's faith.

Let's learn how to believe in the right things.

The antidote to frustration is a calm faith, not in your own cleverness, or in hard toil, but in God's guidance.
–Norman Vincent Peale

1. Analyze what you really believe.

That deep emotional conviction of the presence of a superior reasoning power, which is revealed in the incomprehensible universe, forms my idea of God.
–Albert Einstein

Have you ever thought about what you believe? Many of us go through life thinking we have things figured out. We develop opinions on news and express ourselves on topics at parties. But have we ever really decided what we really believe?

Beliefs are the core of who you are. They determine how you think and act. You need to know your basic self in order to make informed decisions.

That's getting a little philosophical, so let's look at some examples:

Say you're working with an attractive married man 20 years your junior. You spend many hours together on a project and go to lunch and an occasional business dinner. He starts hitting on you, despite the age difference. You feel flattered, but how do you respond?

Or you're driving with friends and your foot gets a little heavy on the gas pedal. When you pull over for the flashing lights, do you lie to the police to avoid the ticket or do you admit what you did?

Maybe you're at a party with friends you think would have nothing to do with drugs. All of a sudden, you have a reefer in your face and everyone around is encouraging you to inhale. What do you do?

All of these have happened to me, so they're not just theoretical.

In each of these instances, you don't have much time to decide. You must respond immediately.

Obviously you can't research online or ask friends and family for advice. That's when you need to have your values and beliefs already settled. You'll be prepared for any dilemma, anytime, anywhere because it's your nature. No need to analyze a situation, determine a correct response, or wish later that you'd reacted differently, because you did the right thing.

Take some time now to think about and write down what you believe. Start with your church's list of beliefs. Go to their website and click About or What We Believe. Read each item and decide if you agree, then write it down.

It's okay if you don't agree with everything your church believes. What is important is that you agree on the fundamentals.

Your list may evolve as you discover more about yourself. Just figure out what you believe and why, so you feel comfortable with who you are and you're prepared for any situation.

2. Have daily devotions.

Three times a day [Daniel] got down on his knees and prayed, giving thanks to his God, just as he had done before.

–Daniel 6:10

We've heard this suggestion many times from pulpits and Sunday school teachers. It always seemed drudgery to me, having to spend a few minutes every morning reading my Bible and praying. I had many more things to do.

Then I discovered what it means. Reading your Bible is God talking to you. Prayer is talking to God. Meditation is listening. With all three combined, you're communicating with God.

You wouldn't think of starting a day without saying good morning to your husband or telling your kids to do well in school. So why would you begin a morning without talking to the one who lives IN you, not just WITH you?

We've all heard super-religious people brag about spending an hour in prayer or reading through the Bible every few months. But when you have sincere devotions, really talking and listening to God every day, you won't need to tell anyone. Your life will show it. You'll become more joyful, more confident, more loving, less judgmental, and generally a better person.

So how do you fit devotions in with everything else? You may not think you can squeeze an extra 10 minutes into your morning. Try setting your alarm to get up a few minutes early just for this.

Start each morning with a devotional book and read the scripture and comments. Then sit quietly and meditate, letting your mind digest it. After doing this for a week, increase the time by a minute or two.

Eventually, you may not need a book of devotions. You can just read a section of the Bible, maybe a chapter or two each day. And meditate while you read and after you're done. Just sit and let your mind figure out what God is saying to you.

Like anything else, it'll take 21 consecutive days for devotion time to become a habit. Try it for three weeks and see the difference it can make in your life.

3. Pray out loud, and not just gimme's.

All who call on God in true faith, earnestly from the heart, will certainly be heard, and will receive what they have asked and desired.

–Martin Luther

In our church, when someone prays, the rest of us listen. Some churches have everyone pray aloud at the same time. If that's your church, you already pray out loud. You just need to do it at home.

So why would praying aloud make a difference? Let's say you pray only in your mind. You start thinking, "Dear God, thank you for all the blessings in my life," and then you slip into, "I can't believe all I have to do today." Then you list everything on your schedule and plan what to wear so you can go from work to errands to dinner with friends. What happened to your conversation with God?

If you're praying aloud, there's less chance that your mouth and your mind will wander. You can keep the conversation going. It's more of a relationship, instead of just something in your head.

So what do we pray about? We all have needs and wants, whether for us or for family and friends. They may involve health, money, education, relationships, or any number of things. And those issues are probably all good. Go ahead and ask God for them, but don't stop there.

Remember when you were a kid and you'd ask your dad for something? Is that all you said? Of course not. You'd talk about other things, tell him what you liked about him, and maybe "kiss up" a little. And the gimme's came after. You didn't focus on what you wanted from him, and you probably didn't ask for everything, just the most important.

Treat your Heavenly Father the same way. Talk to him. Tell him how great he is and thank him for all that he's done for you. He'd like to hear those things.

I found out that God doesn't work on a "multiple-choice" basis. We can't give him our favorite option, then B, C, and D in order of preference. I think he laughs at our ideas. When we offer him choices, God sometimes answers, "None of the above." He comes up with his own solution, usually better than anything we could ever dream.

When my husband was dying of cancer, I prayed and prayed for his healing. I gave God suggestions for ways Bryan could be healed, but God had his own ideas. From the time he was born, God knew how long Bryan would live. God's plan was for me to write about it and help others travelling that road. As much as it hurt, his plan was the best. I wrote *Stepping Through Cancer: A Guide for the* Journey, which has helped hundreds of people going through or caring for others with cancer.

God's answer to my prayers was not in any of the options I offered him. He had something greater in mind, something I would never have thought of. And he's been with me every step of that road.

4. Communicate with God.

Then you will call, and the Lord will answer;
you will cry for help, and he will say: Here am I.
–Isaiah 58:9

What do you think of when you hear the word "pray"? For some, it means kneeling quietly with head bowed and hands folded. For others, it's standing with your face upturned and speaking out loud. Still others think of praying as talking to God and telling him what they want or need in their or others' lives.

Praying is all that and so much more. God wants a relationship with you.

Imagine being married to someone who never talked, only listened. One spouse doing all the talking, and the other with no input. Your husband might be sitting in the house, but you'd know nothing about him, what he thought or liked or hated, how he felt, or what he wanted to do. You might feel unloved, since communication was a one-way street.

Now imagine that relationship with God. You're doing all the talking and not letting him tell you what he's thinking. He may have ideas for you, but you won't take time to listen. And his ideas could be better than yours, but you'll never know.

Try talking *with* God, not *to* him or *at* him. With him. Make it a two-way relationship by taking time to listen to what he has to say to you.

Often, we plan our lives, designing steps to get where we want to go. Then, years down the road, we look back and see that each of those steps got a little farther off the path we planned and now we're nowhere near what we expected.

That's true for me. I planned on marrying my high school sweetheart, travelling with him wherever he was stationed in the Navy, and being a good wife and mother. We never did marry, and here I am decades later, having lived through a divorce, being a single mother, remarrying, and losing a husband to death. None of that was on my wish list.

I learned that life is a journey taken one step at a time. Listening to what God had in mind for me helped me take those steps, even when I had no idea where I would end up.

So how do you listen to God? When you talk with him, make it more of a conversation. Pause between sentences in your prayers. That's when God can interject a thought or an idea.

Maybe you lie awake at night, waiting for your brain to let your body go to sleep. Often, that's when God will give you an inspiration that you were too busy to hear earlier in the day. That's when he'll give me something to write, so I get out of bed and jot it down or it'll be gone by morning.

There was a time when meditation was considered taboo by Christians. However, meditation is just concentrated reflection or contemplation. Nothing bad there. It's just a long pause in conversation for your mind to be open, for the other person to talk. Just so happens that other person is God.

5. Get involved in your local church.

Two are better than one, because they have a good return for their labor: if either of them falls down, one can help the other up. But pity anyone who falls and has no one to help them up.
–Ecclesiastes 4:9-10

Many people are content to go to church only on Sunday morning, if at all, and warm a pew. It's just a place they go out of habit, nothing more. Getting involved seems like something only old folks do. But it's great for younger people, even children.

Being involved is a way to connect with others who share the same beliefs and passions. Not only can you create lasting friendships, but you might also help others in many ways. Offering to usher gives you the opportunity to meet folks as they walk in. Singing in a choir or worship team lets you see all the smiling (or not-so-happy) faces in the congregation.

When my husband was in a serious car accident, our church family rallied around to help us. Choir buddies and others provided food, comfort, medical supplies, and even laid sod in our back yard. Had we not known these folks, we probably wouldn't have asked and would never have received such wonderful gifts.

Church is not a place for perfect people. It's a place for broken people to help each other, a place for imperfect people trying to be better. Finding a home there and getting to know others who've been where you are now, will get you more than you ever give. It's another relationship that's worth the effort to build.

6. Walk with your head high.

> *I will hold my head high*
> *Lift my hands to the sky*
> *Rise above all who try to bring me down*
> *I will hold my head high*
> —**Mark Lee**, Third Day[11]

My niece Georgia was self-conscious as a child. She walked with her head down, staring at the floor, unwilling to make eye contact. Her dad, my brother Butch, told her to lift her head and walk like she belonged. It took a lot of reminding and nudging her chin, but she eventually became confident.

That confidence has stayed with her, and people today are drawn to her, just because she looks like she knows what she's doing. Georgia believes this was the best advice she ever received. It changed her life just as it can change yours.

One friend is overweight but very self-confident, so she doesn't identify with this hint. She has a supportive husband and kids who think she's fabulous just as she is, so she doesn't have any self-doubt. If that's you, thank God for your healthy attitude and move on to another suggestion to work on.

You might think: "I'm not as _____ (fill in the blank: pretty, thin, smart, talented, whatever) as _____ (fill in a name), so I'll just look down. That way, no one will notice me and realize that I'm not as good."

Here's a secret: you *are* good at something. It may be cooking, housekeeping, hair styling, music, art, parenting, or any number of other things.

Stop and think about what you enjoy doing, what you love so much that you'd do it whether or not you got paid. That's probably what you're good at, or could become better if you practiced more. Just because you don't excel in the same areas as someone else doesn't mean you're not good at anything.

Here is a four-step process to help you feel terrific about yourself:

1. Take inventory and discover what you're good at. Write down everything you do today. Then read your list, and when you get to something that makes you smile or feel good inside, that's where you excel.
2. Tell yourself, "I'm good at _____." You'll probably have to say it over and over before you believe it, but it's true.
3. When you walk down the street or enter a room, repeat that in your head. "I am good at _____." It can give you confidence like you never knew. One friend had a hard time getting anywhere on time. When she'd arrive, she would pause before entering the room and say to herself, "I'm late … and I'm *fabulous*." Then she'd swoop into the room with all the confidence in the world. Try it.
4. Let your face reflect how good you feel. Relax those muscles and smile. Holding your head high with a scowl gives the wrong impression, so show off that smile. Poise will radiate from your face and you will look and *be* fabulous.

Being confident doesn't mean believing that you're good at everything. It just not letting the less-than-outstanding things bother you.

I'm not good at writing stories. I can tell jokes and entertain at a party or in a group, but I don't have the imagination necessary to create characters and plots. My ideas help others with their novels, but I don't feel confident enough to write my own.

That won't keep me from writing. I'll do what I'm good at and stretch myself every once in a while. Maybe one day I'll become a best-selling novelist. Probably not, but that won't stop me from writing.

7. Love yourself.

> *Love yourself first and everything else falls into line. You really have to love yourself to get anything done in this world.*
> **–Lucille Ball**

Do you love yourself? If you're like I was, the answer would be NO. I used to think, *No one could possibly love me. I've done so many bad things and been damaged. I don't deserve love from anyone, including myself.*

Here's something you probably already knew but hadn't really thought of: God, the almighty God of the universe, creator of heaven and earth, loves you. *God* loves *you*! So who are you to think you know better than God who is lovable?

There are times when I think that because I'm alone, nobody loves me, so I can't love myself. That's when God comes to me in those prayer pauses and says, "I love you. Don't ever forget that. I love you, and you can love yourself." That gives me courage to face a new day with a smile on my face and my head held high.

I am loved. I love myself. And I can extend that love to others.

> *It is of practical value to learn to like yourself. Since you must spend so much time with yourself you might as well get some satisfaction out of the relationship.*
> **–Norman Vincent Peale**

Chapter 8

BRAIN

*The brain is a wonderful organ; it starts working the moment you
get up in the morning and does not stop until you get into the office.*
–Robert Frost

I was blessed (or cursed) with a high IQ. School was always
easy for me, and I couldn't understand those who had to
study hard just to pass. Eventually, I learned that some
classmates resented me for skewing the grading curve, so I began hedging
my answers to lower my grades and be accepted by my peers. That didn't
make me less smart; it just hid the real me.

As I've aged, my brain has gotten overloaded with so much to
remember and analyze. And meeting many people provided more faces
and names to catalog and recall at a moment's notice. Sad to say, those
results weren't always the best.

One of my favorite ways to greet someone who seems to know me is to say, "I'm sorry. I don't recall your name. I'm Debbie Hardy." They usually respond with, "I know who you are," but then they take the ball and introduce themselves to me—again. Thank you!

Just because our brains are getting older and fuller doesn't mean that we can sit back and let them turn to mush. Here are some ways to keep our minds alert and working well into senior-adulthood.

1. Read or watch news most days, but not at night.

The one function that TV news performs very well is that when there is no news we give it to you with the same emphasis as if it were.

–David Brinkley

It's important to keep up on what's happening in the world and what everyone is talking about. A co-worker got the idea that watching the news was a waste of time. Unfortunately, when meeting prospective clients, she made an ignorant comment about a current event. As a result, those clients called her manager and said, "We like your company and want to do business with you, but not with her. She's an idiot."

Finding out what's happening in your world is easy. There are newscasts, TV channels, and websites devoted to nothing but current events and opinions of them.

No matter what time zone you live in, local television programming usually ends each day with a news broadcast. You'll want to know what happened, but not right before you go to sleep.

My husband and I had a nightly ritual: we always had "snuggle time" before bed. We'd watch whatever cop-and-robber show was on at 9 pm, followed by local news. That provided 90 minutes of people being angry, shooting each other, and dying.

Then we tried to sleep.

Bryan complained every morning of a restless night and horrible dreams. At first we blamed the medications he was taking. But our brains were just processing what we poured into them right before bed.

I was having bad dreams too, but when I stopped watching late-night news, sleep became a welcome, uninterrupted rest. And after Bryan gave up nightly news (which took some convincing on my part), he also could sleep.

So how did we keep up on current events? We watched the news in the morning, which contained the same stories as the night before. And since they weren't at the forefront of our brains when we went to bed, we didn't have unsettling dreams.

2. Learn something every day.

> *I consider that a man's brain originally is like a little empty attic,*
> *and you have to stock it with such furniture as you choose.*
> **–Arthur Conan Doyle**

Once they finished high school, many of my friends swore they'd never take another class. And they kept that promise, which was not good. Their brains never grew past the 18-year-old stage, and they acted like it too.

That statement "If you don't use it, you'll lose it" applies to your brain, but it's easy to get that muscle back in shape. Just like exercise for your body, start slow, build gradually, and you can make amazing improvements.

Many of us spend hours playing games or connecting with others on a computer. Why not spend some of that time training our brains?

Discover a subject you're passionate about or interested in. Search the web for posts, articles, or classes on that topic. Classes might be online, by telephone, or in person. Locate a book to buy or borrow from a library and schedule an hour a day to read.

Magazines are a good source of learning. Your local bookstore probably has a huge section of magazines by topic. Find one that interests you and buy it.

If you're serious about learning, you could attend a conference or audit a class at a local college.

When I began my writing career, there was a lot I didn't know and many folks were farther along on the road to success. At writers' conferences, I was amazed to see faculty members sitting in workshops taught by their peers. These were successful writers, but they knew there could be something of benefit in another class. They weren't too proud to learn more.

I've determined to do the same. No matter what or where I teach, if I get the opportunity to sit and listen to someone else's workshop, I'm there.

Learning is like panning for gold: sometimes all you get are pebbles, things you already know or can't use. Maybe it's fool's gold, something that gets your attention but doesn't work out. But once in a while I come across a valuable nugget, that bit of inspiration that makes a huge difference.

What nuggets can you find today?

3. Play brain games like Sudoku, crossword puzzles.

A man who works with his hands is a laborer; a man who works with his hands and his brain is a craftsman; but a man who works with his hands and his brain and his heart is an artist.
–Louis Nizer

Here's some great news for those who enjoy playing video games: they can actually be good for your brain. Games exercise different parts of your gray matter, whipping it into or keeping it in shape.

For a long time, I played crossword puzzles. Not only did they help my memory by forcing me to recall facts, but they also increased my vocabulary. Until I completed crosswords, I had no idea what a *nene* was or all the ways to spell *emir* and *rani*. But I didn't realize the puzzles were improving my brain until I stopped playing.

When I discovered Sudoku, I quit crosswords cold turkey. Sudoku provided the logic my common-sense mind loved. Spare time was spent filling in those numbers, but I had trouble remembering names and places.

Then I decided to alternate the two games and add a few more. With a combination of Sudoku, crosswords, word searches, and other puzzles, my brain settled into a comfortable system of learn, stretch, and retrieve info quickly.

You can do the same. Find a game you enjoy so you'll play it every day. Then, find a second game and play both. Then add a third.

Just don't play too long. After all, you don't want to ignore other parts of your life. Also, if you're competitive, avoid playing online with others. While it's fun to outdo someone, it can waste more time than it's worth.

I've had to turn off the timer or get rid of high-score screens, just so I don't play endlessly to improve my record. It's addictive to me, so if you have the same problem, beware and take steps to control it. "Everything in moderation" works in all areas of life.

4. Listen to others, but make up your own mind.

A man's brain has a more difficult time shifting from thinking to feeling than a woman's brain does.
–Barbara de Angelis

No one can know everything, not even Albert Einstein. So it's a good idea to get info wherever you can, from friends or others with experience.

To most people, good advice is something you've asked for that agrees with what you think anyway. Conversely, bad advice is something you didn't ask for or that goes against your opinion.

I heard a saying, "Keep an open mind, but not so open that everything falls out." Learn enough to make up your mind, but don't give up your core beliefs.

My husband Bryan watched news channels for hours every day. It's one thing to watch a news PROGRAM, but another to watch a news CHANNEL. Newscasters can only spend so much time saying what happened, and then they begin interpreting the why and the how. You're no longer getting the news; now, you're getting opinions and editorials.

Bryan would get passionate about an issue and take a stance just because someone had a logical argument for it. Unfortunately, he seldom remembered their logic, only their conclusion. He had an opinion but no idea why.

That's when it's good to turn off the input and do some thinking for yourself. Determine your own belief on any topic. When you've analyzed and thought about it, you can explain what you believe, why, and how you came to believe it. You can justify your stance to anyone. It's much better than the I-can-yell-loudest-so-I-must-be right mentality or So-and-So said it, so it must be true.

When you believe, truly believe something, you'll see how settled it can make your life. You don't have to quote the rules or worry about toeing the line. It's a part of you now.

5. Gather information to make educated decisions.

I have a theory about the human mind. A brain is a lot like a computer. It will only take so many facts, and then it will go on overload and blow up.

–Erma Bombeck

Everyone makes decisions: what to wear, who to marry, what career to choose, when to go to bed, how to do anything and everything. The number of options can be overwhelming.

I met a lady who simplified it: no matter how many options there seem to be, you only have two choices: yes and no. A restaurant menu has various entrees, side dishes, and salads. But when you look at one item, the question is, "Yes or No?" Once you've answered that, go to the next item. When you decide on a Yes, you're ready to order.

Same with what to wear, which route to drive, or who to spend time with. Look at each option and ask yourself: "Yes or No?" When deciding on clothing for the day, I pick one item that I really want to wear. That narrows down the rest of the options. Say I want my purple blazer and black slacks. Those eliminate the other blazers and slacks so all I need are a blouse, shoes, and accessories.

Every time you're faced with a decision, make sure you have all the info you need and then look at the options one at a time. If you want to drive a certain route to work, check the traffic report to be sure there's no accident or construction to interfere. Before going to a restaurant, have an idea what you'd like to eat— steak, chicken, or salad entrée—and look only at those items on the menu.

That's also a good way to stick to a diet: make up your mind ahead of time what you'll eat and if you'll have dessert. Then leave room in your calorie count for that.

The bottom line is this: get as much objective information as you can for any decision, especially important, life-changing ones. It's better to find things out before you commit than after you're stuck with a choice you regret.

6. Make lists.

If you're like me, I get hooked into to-do lists, you know. I'll say I checked that off. Okay, I did that. And you have all these things you're doing.

–Jeff Bridges

I can hear it now. "I don't like to make lists." "What, are you OCD or something?" "A list limits what I do."

My husband Bryan felt the same way. He would chuckle when he saw me writing on a piece of paper or crossing something off. And he would roll his eyes when I suggested that he make lists.

Then came the night he complained about my teenaged son temporarily living with us and the problems that created. He went on and on about cleanliness (or lack thereof), laziness, and us not having time alone. I suggested that he write his complaints down to get them out of his head. After thinking about it, he agreed.

When Bryan looked at his list, he said, "Is that all? I thought there was much more than that. I guess I was just letting it spiral out of control by keeping it inside." That's one benefit of making a list—getting your thoughts out so you can look at them objectively.

My friend Allison (she's on the cover) makes a list when she's analyzing a relationship. She divides her paper into two columns titled Pros and Cons, and then adds items as she thinks of them. After a while, it becomes obvious why the relationship should continue or end. And if at some point in the future she might like to have the jerk back in her life, she rereads her list and remembers all the reasons she got rid of him in the first place.

A list can also remind of what needs to be done. To start, write down the obvious items. Add others as you think of them. If you start the list early in the week, you'll have plenty of time to remember all the errands you need to run on Saturday, who to call, or anything else that comes to mind. Another benefit is that you keep your word and do what you promised yourself and others.

After Bryan created that first list, he realized how good it was to have everything written down and not rely on his memory. He then would regularly make a to-do list at breakfast of everything he wanted to accomplish that day.

I prefer to create my list before bed, so my brain doesn't have to work all night remembering what I need to do when I get up in the morning. Having everything written helps me sleep. Who would've thought a list was a good sleep aid?

7. Eat brain food.

Food for the body is not enough. There must be food for the soul.
–Dorothy Day

Eating brain food doesn't mean eating only carrots and fish. We don't need to live like animals, but we must make wise choices about what we put in our bodies.

First, the less processing, the better. Eating raw food is best, followed by lightly-cooked. The worst would be eating out or heat-and-serve at home, where you have no idea what is actually in the food or how it was prepared. Add-water-and-microwave is no better.

One way to avoid processed food is to go "perimeter shopping." When you enter a grocery store, turn right or left and only shop on the outer edges, the perimeter of the building. You'll go through the produce, dairy, and meat departments instead of the prepared foods. You may find the bakery out there as well, but just be conservative about baked goods.

If you research online, you'll find information on which foods are best for your brain and memory. Then choose which to eat. My normal diet plan includes coffee only in the morning, whole grains, fish, eggs, fruit, and salad with spinach and avocado, all of which are reportedly good for mental health.[12]

But even better news is that walnuts, dark chocolate, and cashews are on the positive list, as are peanut butter, cheese and yogurt.[13] Most of these food choices are tasty and not all in the same food group, so we can vary our menu and be smart about it.

Some yogurts with fruit have added sugar to improve flavor. Don't count this kind of yogurt as one of your fruit servings. It's like eating apple-flavored candy instead of an apple or having a banana daiquiri in place of a banana.

Start your day with breakfast, and not just a donut and coffee. Focus on protein, whole grains, dairy, and fruits, but don't overdo it. According to TIME Healthland, "A good meal in the morning can help your body prepare for the day to come, and lower your risk of heart disease, diabetes, and obesity."[14]

Have a salad at least once a day and focus on vegetables and protein for the other meals. Sugar and processed baked goods may give an energy spike, but you come crashing down and then your brain won't be as sharp.

An easy way to decide what to eat is to read the ingredients. If there's anything your mouth can't pronounce, your brain probably doesn't know what to do with it. Stick with simpler foods and you'll be pleased at how you can think and remember better.

8. Control blood sugar spikes.

Foods high in bad fats, sugar and chemicals are directly linked to many negative emotions, whereas whole, natural foods rich in nutrients—foods such as fruits, vegetables, grains and legumes— contribute to greater energy and positive emotions.

–Marilu Henner

I have hypoglycemia. That means that my body doesn't manufacture the right amount of blood sugar (glucose) to function normally. I have to eat frequently to keep my brain working or I get dizzy and shaky. It's also a good excuse to snack, which is my downfall.

Your brain needs a regular supply of glucose to function, so you need to feed your brain every few hours to keep it working well. But avoid sugar or you could have problems.

When you were a kid, did you eat candy when Mom wasn't looking? Remember bouncing off the walls? Well, the same thing happens to adults, although we usually control our wall-bouncing. We get a rush of energy and try to expend it, physically or verbally.

A better idea is to eat a little between meals, maybe a piece of fruit or a handful of nuts, anything around a hundred calories. Your body can digest it easily, and you won't feel that sugar rush.

Your brains tell you what your body needs—you just have to listen. For me, there are times when I want something salty or maybe some chocolate to create endorphins, those feel-good chemicals that reduce pain. If I don't allow myself a small snack to satisfy that need, I'll graze on everything in my kitchen until that desire is gratified.

I used to avoid potato chips and try to eat something healthy instead. First it would be a piece of fruit. When that didn't satisfy, I tried pretzels, then some salted peanuts. I'd even get some chocolate or a scoop of ice cream, because I didn't know what my body needed.

Now, if I get the urge for potato chips, I'll put some in a bowl to keep me from eating the entire bag. That way, I satisfy my craving and get the sensation that my taste buds are looking for without adding hundreds of extra calories.

9. De-stress every day.

Getting stress out of your life takes more than prayer alone. You must take action to make changes and stop doing whatever is causing the stress. You can learn to calm down in the way you handle things.

–Joyce Meyer

Life is stressful, whether you work a 9-to-5 job, run a Fortune 500 company, take care of a parent, or are retired. Many of you work for a difficult boss, put up with lazy co-workers, drive through rush-hour traffic, and or come home to spend an hour cooking dinner before you can sit down. There's always something difficult waiting for you.

One of our biggest stresses can be our finances, which one reason for divorce—usually the lack of money or disagreement on how to spend it. So even if you're able to handle stress from traffic, bosses, or parents, those bills are always in the back of your mind, ready to infect every thought and experience you have.

Just as we need to wake up, eat, and drink every day to survive, we also must de-stress on a regular basis. Dealing with stress can become easier with practice. As you let one stress go, other stresses diminish. Find what helps and then do it every day of your life. (More on that in the next suggestion.)

A doctor might have you take a pill every day to fix something inside your body. This is a prescription to yourself. De-stress once a day for the same reason. If you don't, you're risking your health the same as if you quit taking those prescriptions.

Hopefully, you care enough about yourself to do what's best for you. Some women feel less important than their husbands, children, and everyone else in their lives. They take care of others, but ignore their own needs. If this is you, think how others would cope if you weren't around. Or if the roles were reversed and they had to take care of you.

If not for yourself, de-stress for them. Your loved ones want you around for a long time, so be sure to provide that gift to them.

10. Discover your personal tranquilizer.

If you ask what is the single most important key to longevity, I would have to say it is avoiding worry, stress and tension. And if you didn't ask me, I'd still have to say it.

–George Burns

Playing piano is my tranquilizer. Bryan knew that when I came home from work, sat at my keyboard, and played for a half hour, he should leave me alone. After my "musical Valium®," I was ready to face the rest of the day.

What's your de-stressor? Figure out what makes you feel relaxed or empowered.

Music is soothing, whether you play an instrument, sing with the radio, or just listen on the way home. Loud, pounding rhythms do nothing to calm me down, so I stay away from that kind of music.

But not everyone is the same. Patricia is my opposite—she uses music with a heavy beat to calm herself. Evelyn listens to angry music to release her anger audibly. Rosalee reads a book and loses herself in a character or situation. Lisa sings along with the music of a Christian radio station on her way home from work. That gives her decompression time, so she's ready for husband and kids by the time she reaches the front door.

For some, the trick is exercise. Many of my friends feel better and more relaxed after a workout. When their lives get too busy to get up and move, their minds, attitudes, and bodies can begin to feel sluggish.

If your stress-buster is reading, don't turn to the newspaper. There's so much bad news that could upset you or add to your stress. Instead, take 30 minutes or an hour to lose yourself in a good book or a magazine on a topic you're passionate about. Just give your mind a respite from the daily chaos.

You can also de-stress with a hobby. Find one you love, one that makes you happy, and immerse yourself in it for a few minutes or a few hours every day. Try to make it accessible, not spread out on the dining room table so it has to be put away every night. If your hobby is easily available, you're more likely to give yourself time to enjoy it.

Eating is not a hobby. It could backfire and add unwanted weight and other health issues. That's called emotional eating, and there is an entire industry built around it. And alcohol creates other problems, so don't go there either. Just be aware and look for something else to fill the need.

Try various things to use as a de-stressor until you find one that works. When you can calm yourself down, the rest of your life calms down around you and things are more manageable.

11. Send positive thoughts.

Your body hears everything your mind says.
–Naomi Judd

If you have an itch, your brain tells you to scratch. Or if you need to be somewhere, your brain tells you to go. When you're thirsty, you brain says, "Reach for that glass, take it to the sink and fill it with water. Now drink until I tell you to stop."

It's that simple. Your body does what your brain tells it to. And if your brain is sending negative thoughts, guess how your body is going respond?

Think about the last time you didn't feel well. Maybe you had a headache, a sore muscle, or back spasms. Your brain told you about the pain and you agreed. But if that's all you thought about, the ache got worse. And if you kept thinking about only that, it could become debilitating.

I've watched people do this. They had nothing in their lives but themselves, so all they thought about was what didn't feel right. Every little twinge became a lengthy complaint to me, to their doctor or to the ladies in the dining room of the senior living center. Eventually, people didn't want to visit and listen to all the complaints.

Plenty of young people whine just as much. Maybe it's narcissism or self-centeredness, but they end up much "older" than their years, pushing others away by a constant negative attitude.

What if our brains sent out positive thoughts instead? What if we focused on how good we felt instead of how lousy? What if we told our bodies the pain wasn't too bad? What if?

This worked for me. The women in my family have knees that don't fit together right and hurt when going up or down stairs. When I focused on how bad my knees felt, the pain increased. Eventually I was wearing knee braces every day, propping up my legs whenever possible, and using an ice pack or a heating pad in bed.

One day, I had a conversation with an older family member and listened to her complaining about all her aches and pains. I realized that I was acting the same—and I was 30 years younger!

Mostly I felt good, so I focused on that and my body listened. I got some shoe inserts, which eased the pain and I was able to carry on a normal life, usually without limping, wearing knee braces, or sitting around hurting and feeling sorry for myself. Life is much better now, and my knees don't keep me on the sidelines.

God gave us amazing bodies with the ability to heal from many diseases. That word comes from dis-ease, meaning not comfortable. Even physicians know this, which is why they recommend that we rest, elevate an injury, or use a home remedy much of the time.

Not to say that we can be cured of everything just through positive thinking. But we know the power our minds have over our attitudes, our actions, and our body's functioning.

So why not help our bodies? Think positive thoughts and enjoy a more positive life.

The chief function of the body is to carry the brain around.
–Thomas A. Edison

The human brain is a powerful computer. And the neat part is that we don't have limited memory like a hard drive. Let's take control of our brains and have them work for us. It's an easy choice to make.

To be wholly devoted to some intellectual exercise is to have succeeded in life.
–Robert Louis Stevenson

Chapter 9

DREAMS & WISHES

Destiny grants us our wishes, but in its own way, in order to give us something beyond our wishes.

–Johann Wolfgang von Goethe

*A*s a child, I dreamed of being a ballerina and wearing tutus and tiaras. When the Beatles rose to fame in my teens, my dream shifted to being in a rock band. High school introduced the possibility of writing for a newspaper. And of course, homecoming queen was a dream. Then there's the happily-ever-after we hear about in fairy tales. My Prince Charming finally arrived and we had our "happily" for a few years, but he died before the "ever after."

Why do we give up our dreams and wishes? Maybe it's because they were foolish to begin with and we couldn't really become a superheroor whatever. Perhaps someone told us we could never accomplish our dream and we believed them.

People spend most of their lives working—at a job, in a career, raising a family, being busy. Then there are those who waste time going to a job they hate, dreaming of the day they can walk away and live the life they really want. They're just putting in time until they can move on, although they don't know what the dream of retirement looks like.

A life which is empty of purpose until 65 will not suddenly become filled on retirement.
–Dwight L. Moody

I was the breadwinner in my family, so I figured I'd have to work until I was old enough to retire. No dreams there. But in the back of my mind was the wish to show people how to be happy. My dream included driving to speaking engagements across America. I wanted an RV so I could see the country instead of just the inside of airports and airplanes.

With my first husband, we were busy earning a living and raising two boys, so fulltime travel was out of the question. My second husband wasn't interested in the RV and dismissed my dreams. It was years before my hopes could even be a possibility.

I dreamed of being a speaker, and friends encouraged me to write about my journey through cancer with my late husband. Those two combined to fulfill the dream I'm living today. If I didn't have that wish before I retired, I wouldn't have a reason to get out of bed now. That's what kept me going and keeps me motivated.

You can plan for your dreams and wishes to come true. Here are some steps to help you get there.

1. Set goals.

Learn from the past, set vivid, detailed goals for the future, and live in the only moment of time over which you have any control: now.

–Denis Waitley

Having a goal is like taking aim. If you don't have a target to hit, there's no sense shooting. If you have a two-week vacation and set out to go nowhere, that's where you'll end up. And when you come home, that's another goal—to get back to your own bed.

When I plan a trip, I first determine the destination (my goal). Then I figure out the steps needed to get there. If it's a road trip, I plan how far I'll drive every day, where I'll sleep each night, and how long it'll take to reach my goal. That way, I'll get to Philadelphia to teach at the Greater Philadelphia Christian Writers' Conference or arrive in Boise in time for my speaking engagement.

A goal may include a place, a time, an event, or any number of things. If you're going to a wedding, you probably want to arrive before the ceremony. That's your goal.

But why do we need goals for life? We're fine going to work every day until we either retire or die. Isn't that enough? Maybe it is for you. But you may want to work toward being healthy or saving enough money to pay for retirement instead. Those things don't just happen.

To be valuable, a goal needs to be SMART. They are Specific, Measurable, Attainable, Realistic, and Time-Bound.[15] If you just say, "Someday I want to be a rock star," chances are you'll never get there. But if you say, "I'll get music training and learn everything I can about the industry and selling CD's so I can record within five years," you know what you want to do, how, and by when.

Take some time right now and brainstorm what you'd like to accomplish within a year, five years, or ten years. Nothing is too crazy. Write down everything you've ever dreamed of doing, just to get it out of your brain and on paper.

Now look at the list and pick your top two or three goals. Give it some thought and prayer to determine what you really want to do, the purpose for your life.

Figure out what it would take to achieve each goal and how soon you could accomplish it. Write down what training you'd need, where you'd need to go, and who you know who could mentor you.

If you want to be a movie star, you may need to relocate to Los Angeles. If author is your goal, you probably don't need a college degree, but you might need training and someone to show you the ropes.

Be realistic about what reaching your goal would involve. List each step to get there, including how long it could take and the cost. You may need to research or even attend an introductory class or seminar before you decide.

By now, you may want to give up. But check the list again and see if there's something that lights your fire. What are you passionate about? THAT should be your goal. If it keeps you awake at night or gets you out of bed in the morning, that's your purpose. Stop at nothing to achieve it.

2. Believe in yourself.

Believe in yourself! Have faith in your abilities! Without a humble but reasonable confidence in your own powers you cannot be successful or happy.

–Norman Vincent Peale

You are more amazing than you think. We've been told we were special since Dr. Seuss helped build up our self-confidence. But somewhere along the way, we gave up. Maybe we attempted something and didn't succeed, so we never tried again. Or we shared our dream with someone and they laughed, so we quit.

When I was six, I saw "The Nutcracker" and wanted to be a ballerina. My sister, just a few years older, laughed and said I would never make it. So I gave up that dream. In fact, it was years before I tried to dance or even tapped my feet to music.

The main thing keeping you from believing you can do something is your mind. So change your mind. Start telling yourself out loud and in writing that you can do what you want. It may take time to prove to yourself and to others that you can do it.

Just take it one step at a time.

If you think you can or you think you can't, you're right.
–Henry Ford

Have you ever seen live crabs in a bucket? Logic would say that they could climb up on each other and eventually get out. But the crabs won't escape, even without a lid. When one gets a leg up, other crabs pull him back down. They prevent each other from fleeing.

Don't be a crab and don't hang around other crabs! Run from anyone who would pull you down and keep you from attempting or achieving your goals. You may need to leave old friends and find new ones who will support your life change. Trust me, it'll be worth it.

When I started writing, I found a nearby writers critique group whose members helped me get better instead of telling me to give up. Look around and find someone who can do the same for you. Then go for it. It's your dream, so no one can live it for you.

3. Get out and play.

The true object of all human life is play. Earth is a task garden; heaven is a playground.

–Gilbert K. Chesterton

Play is fun. If you don't believe that, you haven't played or watched a child play in a while. Think back to when you were on summer break from school. What did you look forward to doing every day? Play! That's what kids do, and they're good at it.

Of course, there are bullies who try to rob your fun, and controllers who decide how everybody is going to play, taking the joy out of it. But play is mostly fun.

Why did we stop playing? Maybe we "grew up" and didn't feel that having fun was appropriate anymore. Perhaps someone told us we were too old to be childish or that playing was just for kids.

My dad felt that if you were playing, you weren't studying or working or doing something productive. He firmly believed that fun was a waste of time. Oh, there were times we would set up the badminton net or Ping-Pong table at a family get-together. But most of the time, we didn't play.

So how, when, and where can we play?

First, find friends to play with. Things are more fun with someone you like.

Second, find something you like to do. I have a friend in her mid-sixties who bowls on two leagues, plays drop-in volleyball, and golfs when the weather cooperates. She was on a roller-hockey team, but had to quit when her knee gave out last year. She does each activity with a different group of friends, and loves every minute.

I'm part of a group of ladies with season tickets to the Colorado Rockies. Even though we're watching baseball and not playing it, the activity is great. And it's fun, whether the Rockies win or lose.

Maybe your fun is Community Theater, camping, or bicycling at a nearby park. Whatever makes you smile and feel good, do it with friends.

Laughter is good for you, which has been proven by many scientific studies.[16] In fact, when I did an online search for "laughter is good for you," I got almost 27 million hits! A good belly laugh can keep you healthy and happy for several days, and may even be able to hold off infection or disease. And it's hard to play and have fun without laughing.

Fun doesn't just happen. You have to plan it. So think of what you'd like to do, call someone to join you, and go do it.

A friend just called and asked if I'd like to join her at a Christian concert. I'll write more tomorrow, but tonight I'm going to have fun. How about you?

4. Hold onto your dreams.

The future belongs to those who believe in the beauty of their dreams.
–Eleanor Roosevelt

We all had dreams at some time in our lives. One of my friends wanted to walk on the moon; another wanted to discover a cure for cancer. A third was performing in local theater and planning to be a movie star.

Some of them worked hard to make their dreams come true. But for most of my friends, life intervened and they ended up just earning a living and gave up those dreams.

So how can you hold onto a dream? Here are five ways:

1. Don't let life or anyone make you give up.
2. Write down your dream. If it's on paper, it's more real than just in your head. Put it someplace you'll see it often, not in a drawer or a file on your computer.

3. Write down steps needed to accomplish it. You may be able to complete some of them easily. God tends to prepare us for whatever he wants us to do, so our training can be in different ways.

4. Ask God what he wants. Perhaps you've been dreaming about an Academy Award for acting, but maybe that's not where he wants you. Chances are, things you've experienced have moved you closer to your dream.

5. Don't give up. I did that for 40 years and regretted it. I resented my family for interfering and myself for not doing something about it. During all that time, God was tutoring me. I didn't realize it until much later, but it's unmistakable.

When you look at all you've lived through, you could be amazed at how much you've learned. And you're probably a step or two closer to your dream than you thought.

So keep that dream alive. It's your reason for living.

5. Live your dream.

All our dreams can come true, if we have the courage to pursue them.
–Walt Disney

Walt Disney was a master at creating dreams and making them come true. His dreams became Disneyland and the Disney Empire. Within those magical worlds, he created dreams the rest of us can share. Perhaps you imagined yourself in Cinderella's castle, dancing with Prince Charming. Many brides have their dream weddings in that very castle.

Why do we share Walt's dreams but won't make our own come true?

Well, it's time to live your dreams. Now is the day to work toward what you've wanted but never achieved. If you need it, you now have permission to be selfish in that regard.

In the last suggestion, we looked at what you wanted to do and how to get there. Now, think about how you'll feel when your dream comes true. That's what we want to achieve.

Close your eyes and imagine living your dream. How do you feel? Who's around and what are they doing? That feeling is what you're really looking for. Put yourself in that situation one step at a time.

If you dreamed of a million-dollar house, what part of that do you really want? A maid? Manicured lawn? Parties? Mortgage payment and utility bills? All that carpet to vacuum? Maybe not, but you can realize little pieces of it. Create landscape one plant at a time. Get rid of some of your "stuff" to make your house feel bigger. And have friends over and host your own parties.

Maybe you dreamed of being famous. There are ways to use social media or make videos and post them to show the world. You don't need a motion picture studio to make you a star. Just be sure you're ready to live with fame.

I wanted to be Miss America. I really wanted people to notice my beauty. Didn't happen. So instead of a crown, I have my Queen of Resilience tiara that sets me apart and makes little girls want their pictures taken with me. And when folks see me wearing that tiara, they notice, smile, and want to talk with me. I'm satisfied.

For now, fake it till you make it. Act as if your dream has come true. I acted as if I were a bestselling author and famous speaker before I really was. Maybe you shouldn't hire a limo driver and hit every red carpet in town, but you can get the feeling, even if only a tiny bit.

Make your dream happen, starting today.

6. Make a Bucket List.

Regret for the things we did can be tempered by time; it is regret for the things we did not do that is inconsolable.

–Sydney J. Harris

There's a movie called "The Bucket List," in which two old guys don't have much life left but there's are still more to do. They make a list of everything they want to accomplish before they kick the bucket and then they do them.

After my husband Bryan was diagnosed with cancer, we spent part of each day writing down everything we wanted to do when his cancer went into remission. Although we had been married for years, there were things we'd planned do "someday" but never got around to.

Unfortunately, we never got the opportunity. He died three months after diagnosis.

So I made another list—just for me. I wrote down things like be a motivational speaker, play piano professionally, travel, get season tickets to the Colorado Rockies, and wear a tiara. They've all been crossed off, so I added more.

When my kids were young, we sat down as a family and made a sort-of Bucket List. We'd take turns and tell where we wanted to go. We put every suggestion on the list, no matter how trite or outlandish. My younger son said, "Go to McDonald's." No surprise there. And for his next turn he added, "Get a [McDonald's] McRib sandwich." We put both on the list, plus everyone else's ideas.

The list hung on the refrigerator. Whenever we wanted to go to dinner, plan an event, or take a vacation, we checked the list for something we really wanted to do, and crossed it off. When the list dwindled, we held another family meeting and wrote another list.

What's on your Bucket List? Get a piece of paper, a white board or a document on your computer. Write anything your brain thinks of, even if it's silly. This is true brainstorming.

List everything, from trying out a new restaurant to cruising the Mississippi on a steamship or visiting Paris. Maybe you'd like to go to the moon. Well, you could find a rocket simulator to give you the same feeling.

When planning an evening out, time with friends, a vacation or a menu, check your list. It may jog your memory to try something new. And you could find more satisfaction from your list than doing the same things again and again.

Don't forget to include family. No one on their deathbed ever said, "I wish I had worked longer hours." More often, they'd say, "I wish I had spent more time with my family." This is one way to limit your regrets.

Decide what you want, then do it. Simple as that.

7. Check your Bucket List often.

As you grow older, you'll find the only things you regret are the things you didn't do.

–Zachary Scott

We tend to lament some things we've done. We may wish we made better decisions, especially in our youth. But we can also regret things we never got around to. There's always something that we didn't accomplish.

So how do we minimize the number of regrets? Hang your Bucket List where you'll see it every day. Any time you need an idea for something to do or someplace to go, refer to the list. That's all it takes. A quick look. That list holds dreams and ideas you had at one time but may have forgotten.

This hint sounds a little too easy. Well, it is easy, like reading the newspaper every morning or checking your calendar. Just having a newspaper or a calendar doesn't mean you'll read it or check it every day. Add checking your Bucket List to your morning routine.

If you think of another item to add, write it down as the idea comes or you'll forget. I learned that the hard way. I never did remember what I was excited about, so it never made it to my list. When I think of it, I'll let you know.

8. Have a purpose, a reason to get out of bed.

Life must be lived and curiosity kept alive. One must never, for whatever reason, turn his back on life.

–Eleanor Roosevelt

What gets you out of bed in the morning? For years, what got me up was my alarm clock and a paycheck to keep a roof over our heads. When I didn't have to go to work, it was usually "Mom, tell him to stop touching me!" that roused me from slumber. But that wasn't enough to make me want to jump out of bed.

Maybe it's the same for you. There's got to be more. If you're one of the lucky ones who loves their jobs, be thankful for that. However, once that job ends, what then?

A former co-worker retired to get away from the job. However, he had no plans for the rest of his life. When I asked how he spent his days now, he said, "Well, I drink coffee and watch television. And I take the dog for a walk." That sounds like a VERY boring life, and someone I don't want to be around.

I tell people retirement isn't what you think. If you are going to sit around and waste your life, you can only golf so much. To stay young, you have to stay in the mix.

–Ron Rice

What are you passionate about that keeps the fire going after you've punched out at work? Discover your passion by looking at what you're interested in or what you talk about, watch, or do day after day. It may be teaching music, playing baseball, volunteering at a food bank, or another hobby.

Once you've found your passion, find a way to keep it alive and a place to work on it regularly. It's also easier to stay committed if you share it with someone. Talk a friend into joining you or find a friend already doing it and join them.

Too often, people retire from a job and have no reason for living. But if you've been developing your passion, it's easy for you to expand the number of hours you work at it. Instead of being just a weekend hobby, it could become a part-time/volunteer job and a great reason to get out of bed.

Wendy loves babies but wasn't blessed with any of her own. She began volunteering in a hospital's neonatal unit, just holding and rocking babies to give them human interaction. When retirement came along, she increased the number of hours to hold little ones. And her life now is happier than it ever was when she got paid.

Finding your passion will not only give you something to do; it can also prolong your life. When you look forward to how you'll spend each day, your life continues to have meaning. See what you can and want to do, for yourself and for others.

Life is really worth living. Find your life's purpose and live it.

Well, I think some people are very happy in retirement. And in a year and a half I'm going to see how happy I feel in retirement. I'm just going to not work quite so hard, but I'll continue to write as long as God gives me breath.

–Jan Karon

BODY

Everybody needs beauty as well as bread, places to play in and pray in, where nature may heal and give strength to body and soul.
–John Muir

My body is not a Size 2 and probably will never even come close. In fact, I haven't worn a Size 2 since I *was* 2! I've gone through many diets and yo-yoed down and up more times than I care to remember. The clothes in the middle of my closet are my current size, while there are "fat clothes" in bags and "skinny clothes" on other racks. I wish I could fit into the smaller sizes, but I keep the larger ones around just in case I expand into them.

Most women are not content with their bodies. We tend to wish our hips were smaller, our boobs bigger (or smaller), or our tummies less poochy. But that's not as important as making sure everything is running as well as it can.

I'm glad some guys prefer women with curves. My husband Bryan loved my "round" body and didn't want it any other way. I finally admitted that I'm larger than I'd like to be, but I'm okay with it. There are clothes that complement my shape, so I double-check my mirror, front and back, to be sure I look fabulous before I leave home.

No matter how beautiful you may be, your insides need to be as healthy as you look on the outside. You don't want to be like cotton candy that is light and fluffy when it's first made, but slowly collapses because there's nothing sturdy holding it together. Eventually it looks like a lump of dust bunnies.

Here are some ways to improve the condition of your body by being healthy, eating well and in correct proportions, and adding movement to your day.

Chapter 10

HEALTH

A healthy outside starts from the inside.
–Robert Urich

y family has a legacy of poor health. Not sure if it's the genes or the environment we lived in. With limited income, we ate a lot of pasta, potatoes, and bread.

I do remember a can of bacon grease that Mom used to fry almost every meal. She would put a glop of that stuff in a skillet and add the meat. Everything tasted delicious, but it wasn't exactly healthy.

And I don't recall going to a doctor or a dentist just for a checkup. When we had a toothache or something physically wrong that didn't clear up in a few days, we'd get to see a professional. With six kids and a father who earned a low wage, that was the only option.

Fortunately, I worked many years for a company that provided very good medical and dental insurance, so my kids got regular checkups.

Good health is more a matter of prevention than medication. In fact, it costs much less and is less painful to prevent a condition than to treat it. Here are some suggestions to keep yourself and your family as healthy as possible.

1. Take care of your health.

> *The wish for healing has always been half of health.*
> **–Lucius Annaeus Seneca**

Surprising as it may be, your doctor is not in charge of your health. You are. Medical personnel can only recommend or prescribe things for you. It's up to you to eat healthy, exercise, and follow their suggestions.

Let's talk about that old adage, "An apple a day keeps the doctor away." Well, an apple doesn't really keep anyone away. The quote dates from the 19th century, when doctors made house calls if someone was sick. Eating fresh fruit, or just eating sensibly, could keep you healthy and reduce the need for a doctor to visit.

The same applies today—if you eat more fresh fruits, vegetables, and non-processed foods, you're more likely to remain healthy and not need to pay a visit to the doctor. The important word here is "pay," It's one of those no-brainer things that we tend to ignore, but it's never too late to start.

I lived in a small town with an old country doctor. He was known and loved by almost everyone. There was one rule about which he was adamant: if he prescribed something for a patient but they didn't follow through, they would not be allowed back to his office for the same complaint. His receptionist was instructed to follow that rule without exception.

One lady had been fighting an infection for a week and had already been to the doctor once. She showed up at his office, hoping to see him again.

"What did the doctor tell you to do the last time you were in?" the receptionist asked.

"He gave me this prescription and told me to gargle, rest and drink lots of liquids."

"And did you do that?"

"No. I didn't have time to get the prescription filled and I hate to gargle. I need something else."

"I'm sorry," the receptionist replied, "but the doctor refuses to see you. Since you didn't believe what he told you at the first appointment, he won't let you waste his time again. You'll have to find a new doctor."

The woman pursed her lips, muttered a few obscenities, and walked out. But it makes sense—if you know what to do and don't do it, you have no excuse for poor health.

As we age, our bodies quit working as well as when we were young. This is normal, but it may happen so gradually that we don't notice. When our eyes start to blur, we realize that they're getting older, so we have them checked and buy glasses. Why can't we do the same when our bodies start to "blur" or act less efficiently?

It's important to be aware of how things are supposed to perform compared to how they work today. Then, if a change becomes noticeable or bothers you, talk with your doctor about it. Some things are normal aging and some are not. Having crow's feet around your eyes is normal. A drooping eyelid is not. A sluggish metabolism may be normal but constipation is not. Pain is also a sign that something is wrong.

One friend was having trouble with her hip. It just didn't feel right and hurt a little, but she thought it was just age or arthritis and that she'd get used to it. When she was at the doctor for a different issue, she mentioned the pain. Upon examination, he determined that her hip joint needed to be replaced. After surgery, she felt much better and wondered why she put up with it for so long. She is now enjoying better movement and less pain.

The same is true of cataract surgery and many other procedures that can improve the quality of our lives. The longer you wait, the longer you put off the comfort you could enjoy.

Of course, you may want to get a second or third opinion before agreeing to surgery. Get all the information you can to make the best decisions for your health.

2. Get regular medical and dental checkups.

It takes more than just a good-looking body. You've got to have the heart and soul to go with it.

–Epictetus

Getting regular checkups may seem obvious, especially if you have a dental or health care plan that includes free examinations. A lot of plans have no copay for annual exams. If it's free, why wouldn't we do it?

My obese mother had her first heart attack at the young age of 49, and was physically disabled until her death 14 years later. I was afraid I'd follow in her footsteps. So now I have all my numbers checked regularly and follow the suggestions my doctor gives to maintain my health.

Believe it or not, the Mayo Clinic has determined that poor oral health can affect your overall health.[17] Not only can it lead to gum disease, but it has been linked to many illnesses. And some conditions might reduce the amount of saliva in your mouth, needed to wash away bacteria. Certain diseases could lower your body's resistance to infection, possibly making oral health problems more severe.

As women, we tend to take care of everyone else, but not ourselves. When an airplane prepares for takeoff, the flight crew gives instructions for proper use of oxygen masks in case of emergency. "Secure your own mask before helping a child or others around you." They know that if you pass out from lack of oxygen, you can't help anyone else, and others may suffer as a result. In reality, we must see to ourselves first or there will be nothing to give those we love.

To be sure you get regular checkups, put reminders on your calendar or make appointments a few months in advance. And when the time comes, show up.

No one can make you take care of yourself. It's entirely up to you, so if you want to live long and prosper, you know what to do.

3. Follow your doctor's instructions.

Healing is a matter of time, but it is sometimes also a matter of opportunity.
–Hippocrates

Doctors have the training and medical knowledge necessary to diagnose and treat conditions and diseases. If you're not a doctor, you probably don't have the education to act as one, even for yourself.

An older friend loves to say, "I know my body better than he does." What she doesn't realize is that she has gotten used to how her body behaves, even when it's bad. Her doctor probably knows how her body is *supposed* to act and what changes need to be made. She just doesn't want someone telling her to exercise and drink more water.

A few years ago, there were commercials showing doctors in lab coats trying to play basketball, drive a semi, and run a crane at a construction site. The point was that your doctors don't do your job, so don't try to do theirs. In the medical field, doing your own diagnosing and treating is called being non-compliant.

I tried to get this message through to my husband and my sons. They would complain about an ache or pain for which I had recommended some treatment, such as a nap, a pain reliever, or propping up a foot. I'd ask them if they did what I told them. If the answer was Yes, they got all the sympathy and care they wanted. If not, I told them there was no sympathy, since it was their choice to continue to feel rotten.

There are times when you might not trust your doctor's judgment. Maybe he told you something you didn't want to hear, or she's focused on getting you to follow a plan that you don't want to. That's okay. We can't agree on everything.

You could always ask for a second opinion. I once overheard a conversation:

Patient: *"Doc, I don't like your diagnosis. Can I get a second opinion?"*
Doctor: *"Sure. You're ugly, too!"*

Okay, that's a little off the subject, but most doctors won't mind if you get a second opinion. Be careful not to keep shopping around until you hear what you want. If ten people tell you you're sick, you better go lie down.

But a second opinion could increase your options for treatment. My husband's cancer appeared to be inoperable, but not all the doctors agreed. One surgeon scheduled a PET scan to verify. As it turned out, his cancer was untreatable, but it was comforting to know that we did everything possible.

It helps to have someone with the patient at appointments. The patient is focused on what's wrong and getting better. A friend can be objective, ask questions, and take notes on what the doctor says to refer to later.

If you have a chronic (ongoing) condition, write down questions you'd like to ask and take the list with you. There's nothing more frustrating than having your doctor say, "Do you have any more questions?" and your mind goes blank when you know there was something you wanted to ask. Write down your doctor's answer so you'll have the info when you need it.

4. Monitor your blood pressure.

Cheerfulness is the best promoter of health and is as friendly to the mind as to the body.
–Joseph Addison

My family has a history of high blood pressure. I thought it was weight-related until I lost a bunch of weight and still had high blood pressure. Although disappointed, I continued to take a lower dose of prescribed medication.

Use the blood pressure machine in the local pharmacy if you want. I'm not too crazy about letting the world know my statistics, so I have a small monitor at home. I keep it in the kitchen, so it's handy whenever I need it. Your doctor can recommend the best brand for you.

Find out from your doctor what your blood pressure should be. If your numbers are way above or below those, talk with your doctor about it to determine how to get it to normal.

There is no shame in taking medications to become or stay healthy. The shame is in not doing something to prevent bad consequences.

5. Keep your cholesterol in check.

You know, all that really matters is that the people you love are happy and healthy. Everything else is just sprinkles on the sundae.
–Paul Walker

High cholesterol means that your arteries are becoming clogged with sediment or plaque that can restrict blood flow.[18] If allowed to accumulate, it could lead to heart disease, blood clots, even a heart attack. Maintaining a healthy cholesterol level can delay or prevent this from happening.

This one is a little harder to keep track of. In-home monitors can be pricey, so a regular visit to the doctor is in order. He can tell if you need to do something about your numbers.

Here's another case where my family history includes high cholesterol, which I thought was connected to being overweight. Not so. I take less medication now that I weigh less, but will probably continue to take something to control my cholesterol for the rest of my life.

6. Take appropriate prescriptions and over-the-counter medications.

Give a man health and a course to steer, and he'll never stop to trouble about whether he's happy or not.
–George Bernard Shaw

Medications can make the difference between living a healthy life and just existing. Some meds are prescribed by your doctor while others are available on a shelf. That doesn't mean that one is good and the other bad. It just means that some are controlled.

Be sure to read the instructions and take only the recommended dosage. You may think that if one pill helps, two will work twice as well. Not necessarily so. Some medications can be toxic if taken in larger doses. One friend was taking an aspirin daily to reduce the chance of blood clots. He doubled the dose and ended up with an ulcer from over-medicating.

Let your doctor know every medication you take, including vitamins, over-the-counter pills, and food supplements. Mixing meds can have negative side-effects, even when each one is safe by itself.[19] Or they may counteract each other, so neither one does what it's supposed to. Your doctor will know which drugs work well together and which should not be combined.

Keep a list of all the medications you take, preferably in your purse or wallet. If you have a phone that allows you to type lists or reminders, add this info. It could come in handy when you need to give the info to a doctor or nurse, especially when you make an unscheduled trip to the Emergency Room.

My mom used to brag that she took her entire stash of medications along to doctor's appointments. He would read the labels, nod, and comment that she was doing the right thing. Then came the day when Mom fell, hit her head, and had to go to the ER. She didn't have a list and had a hard time remembering all the pills she took. The next day, she typed them into her smart phone.

When you find the right combination of meds to feel your best, stick with it. The number of pills is not important. What is important is that your body is functioning the best it can. I've known some folks who didn't like to take pills, so they stopped. And they suffered the consequences: one friend had a heart attack, one suffered with terrible allergies, and a third friend's cancer returned.

For me, if taking a few pills in the morning means that I'll feel better and stay alive longer, I'm all for it. I just need to be sure to have enough water to wash them all down. Once, I wasn't thinking and popped the pills in my mouth at breakfast. The only liquid I had on hand was hot coffee, which I tried to gulp. Let's just say it wasn't a pretty sight. Now, I always make sure I have water or juice nearby before I take my meds.

One last note here: my friend Rosalee suggests that you "Bury your fish or they'll revisit you all day long." That means take your fish oil or garlic capsules before eating or you'll burp them the rest of the day. This is true—I learned it the hard way.

7. Know your BMI.

The greatest weapon against stress is our ability to choose one thought over another.

–William James

For years I would jokingly tell people, "I'm not overweight. I'm just under-tall!" I was the ideal weight if I were six-foot-four. Unfortunately, my five-foot-two frame was a little chunky.

Pinch an inch. Squeeze your "love handles" just above the waist or your "bat's wing" on your upper arms. If you get an inch or more between your fingers, you may want to take action.

Body Mass Indicator (BMI) compares your weight to your height and shows if you're underweight, healthy, overweight, or obese. It isn't foolproof, but it is a good indicator of your health.

The National Institutes of Health is a great source for anything to do with your body. On their website, they explain how to figure your BMI [20]:

1. Measure your height in inches and your weight in pounds.
2. Multiply your weight by 703.
3. Divide that answer by your height.
4. Divide that answer by your height one more time.

Here's the chart to know where your BMI falls:

- Below 18.5 = Underweight
- 18.5-24.9 = Healthy
- 25.0-29.9 = Overweight
- 30.0-39.9 = Obese
- Over 40 = Extreme or high-risk obesity

When you plan a trip, whether to the grocery store or to a family reunion, you may know where you want to go, but you also need to be sure of where you are starting from. That's what the BMI indicates on your road to good health—where you are today. No matter what the number is, at least now you know what you're dealing with.

The first time I learned my BMI, I was shocked that the number indicated that I was obese. That was the motivation I needed to do something. When I lost weight, went down several dress sizes, and recalculated my BMI, I was surprised that I was still considered overweight. I thought I looked and felt pretty good, but the number said otherwise.

I may not be perfect, but I'm still working toward it. And knowing my BMI tells me that I'm on the right road.

Your health is totally up to you. Doctors can give you prescriptions, suggestions, and exercise programs, but it's you implement them. Keep at it.

Rest when you're weary. Refresh and renew yourself, your body, your mind, your spirit. Then get back to work.
–Ralph Marston

Chapter 11

EATING

For the first 50 years of your life the food industry is trying to make you fat. Then, the second 50 years, the pharmaceutical industry is treating you for everything.

–Pierre Dukan

My heritage is fat. When Mom had her first heart attack at the age of 49, she weighed about 200 pounds. After the doctor put her on a strict diet, she lost some of that, but never really got to a healthy weight.

Before the heart attack, Mom spent a decade working at a bakery. Besides having all those baked goods at her fingertips, she brought leftovers home almost every night. We never lacked sweets in our house, and it showed on our hips and bellies. Mom believed that food fixed everything, so there was always more than enough to eat.

Naturally, I followed suit as an adult. The best and worst thing I did after high school was go to college. It was best because it opened the door to a new world; it was worst because of the all-you-can-eat meals—21 of them every week! I added far more than the "Freshman Fifteen," the 15 pounds most students put on during freshman year.

I've tried many diets, some sensible and some crazy. One of them was so strict that I could only eat one hard-boiled egg for breakfast. Lunch was a small piece of meat and half an apple, and dinner was a piece of lettuce. Not exactly the healthiest diet and I was hungry all the time.

By Saturday, I wanted to eat anything within reach. Lunch's instructions were to make a fruit salad, put anything in it, and eat as much as I wanted. So I cut up an apple, a banana, a peach, some strawberries and some grapes. Then, I added other things I wanted: pecans, coconut, whipped cream, and maraschino cherries. What a fabulous fruit salad, but it had WAY more calories than I should have eaten.

When we stop to think about it, eating sensibly isn't that hard. It's all a matter of moderation, not gorging yourself on something you crave or that looks or smells really good.

Here are some ways we can eat what we want and not suffer as a result.

1. Eat well.

A woman should never be seen eating or drinking, unless it be lobster salad and Champagne, the only true feminine and becoming viands.

–Lord Byron

Eating well doesn't mean eating rich foods at fancy restaurants. It means eating what is best for your body. I'm not saying to eat only apples, nuts, and tree bark. Just be sensible.

My dad used to say, "Most people eat to live. I live to eat." And his body certainly showed it: he was obese and had numerous health problems. After he was diagnosed as borderline diabetic, Mom cooked healthier meals and cleared all the junk food out of the house.

Dad fought Mom's efforts. "What? Are you trying to starve me? This stuff tastes like cardboard!" He lost weight, but he complained all the time. Because he was a mean person to begin with, Mom gave up. Dad put all the weight back on and his medical problems returned.

Eating well is easy and can be tasty. The Number One fact to remember is: The more processed a food is, the worse it is for you. We know raw fruits and vegetables contain more nutrients than canned, cooked or frozen. The same goes for breads: the more whole grains, the better. Unbleached and unrefined flour is better than the over-processed kind.

Many diet plans send meals to your door and all you have to do is eat them. What they don't tell you up front is that you must supplement their meals with fresh produce. And you may not learn how to prepare your own food, so you'll keep buying theirs.

My friend Brenda (she's on the cover) did so well on a diet plan that she was on their commercials for several years. She shared their secret with me: the food they sent was a main dish only. She had to fill her plate three-quarters full of salad or other vegetables and have fruit for dessert and snack. Anyone can do that without spending hundreds of dollars for a program.

Simplicity is the key to eating healthy. Find meals and recipes that allow you to make dishes from scratch. If you work all day, you could to use a crockpot or have a salad for dinner, so you don't have to wait hours to eat.

2. Know your portions. You don't need to clean your plate.

I have never developed indigestion from eating my words.
–Winston Churchill

Most people—myself included—can't judge a portion just by looking at it. I think we're trained to over-fill our dishes. We see huge portions at restaurants and copy that at home. Sad to say, the more food a restaurant puts on our plate, the more we like it and the more often we eat there and give rave reviews.

When I was young, my parents lectured us to clean our plates before leaving the table. Many times, they dished up too much food and I overate just so I could leave. I decided to change the rules for my kids. If they served themselves, they should only take what they wanted. But they were required to clean their plates and not waste anything. If someone else served the food, that person had no idea how hungry my boys were, so they didn't have to eat it all.

I tried to teach one son not to clean his plate when he ate out. I told him, "Look for the biggest person in the restaurant. That's the one they're catering to. They dish up enough food to satisfy him or her so they won't get complaints."

My overweight son's response was, "What if you're the biggest person in the restaurant?"

"That should tell you something. Maybe you're eating too much."

Unfortunately, that's how we tend to serve our meals at home. We heap on the food, especially at holidays, to be truly satisfied. Then, we follow Mom's advice and clean our plates. Unfortunately, my mom's words rang in my ears when I was a young mother, and *I* ended up eating all the food my sons left uneaten. After gaining the extra pounds to show for it, I had to take drastic measures to lose them.

Also, our metabolism slows down with age,[21] making it harder to maintain a healthy weight. We must do something different to watch our weight.

Here are some ideas to cut down on the amount we eat.

1. To be sure of portion amounts, get a food scale and a calorie chart in a book or online. Then, weigh your food before you eat it. Your calorie chart will indicate how much a portion should be, so get a true picture of what you're putting in your mouth.

2. When eating out, divide your food in half at the beginning of the meal, so you're not tempted to clean your plate. Ask for a to-go box for the half you won't eat. Then, eat only what is left on your plate and take the rest home. You'll be surprised at the amount of food it *doesn't* take to satisfy your hunger.

3. There are times when a dish is so good that you'll want seconds even though it would be more than a single serving. When that happens, either take a few more bites to satisfy that craving or find something with fewer calories to crunch, like fresh veggies.

4. Whenever I tell myself I can't have something, that's what my mind and body crave, and I end up grazing on everything available to satisfy that desire. Rather than denying myself now and then overeating later, I may eat half a cookie or a small piece of dessert for that sweet tooth,

5. Another way to convince your stomach you've had enough is to chew your food slowly. This allows your taste buds to savor the flavor and enjoy it more, instead of having just a passing taste. And when your stomach sends the message that it's full, you can stop without extra mouthfuls already on their way down to stuff into your stomach.

3. Have nutritious snacks.

You can tell a lot about a fellow's character
by his way of eating jellybeans.
–Ronald Reagan

Do you ever get the three-o'clock munchies? Or feel hungry mid-morning and want just a little something to eat? We all have those times when our bodies need a boost of energy. But how we get that boost can make a big difference.

We could grab the nearest salty, sweet, or carbohydrate treat, like a candy bar, and get an instant jolt. But the boost wears off and we're left feeling more tired than before. Plus, we might gain extra weight if we do it too many days in a row. Not to mention the guilt we'd feel for having "cheated."

Instead of something sweet or salty, try something high in fiber. Carrots, celery sticks, cut-up cauliflower, or cucumber slices feed your desire to crunch while reducing the need for "crunches," those hold-in-your-stomach sit-ups. It takes planning to have these on hand and ready to eat, but it's well worth it.

You could snack on fruit, like an apple or a banana. Smear some peanut butter, which is high in protein, to keep you satisfied longer. Cheese is also a good snack and has calcium to help strengthen your bones.

Your metabolism is constantly trying to regulate your digestion. When you don't eat for a long period of time, your body slows into starvation mode.[22] Then, when you do eat, your metabolism doesn't speed up immediately to digest properly and you could add a few pounds.

You're much better off eating a little bit every few hours to keep your metabolism at a consistent level.

4. Eat popcorn—it's high in fiber and filling.

The laziest man I ever met put popcorn in his pancakes so they would turn over by themselves.

—W. C. Fields

Popcorn is one of the few ideal foods. By itself, it's low in calories and carbohydrates. The problems come when you cook it in oil or drown it with butter or caramel. Those add unneeded calories, not to mention greasy fingers.

If you're like me, you can't go to a movie without having popcorn. And I especially like to go to theaters where you put the butter on yourself. Well, not really on yourself—on your own popcorn. I tend to over-pump and make it extra buttery.

When I was young, we had a neighbor from France who had never had popcorn before emigrating. Sue wanted to please her American husband and make some for him. She came to our door one day, crying. "I don't know what happened," she said. "My husband loves the popcorn, so I boil and boil it in water, but it didn't get all white and fluffy like yours. What did I do wrong?"

If popcorn was really cooked in water, it would be lower in calories. Air-popped is very healthy, although dry and tasteless. I once had my own air-popper and used it very seldom. It seemed to be a waste of a perfectly good snack.

Then I realized that, just like the "Two Fat Ladies" from PBS, butter makes anything taste better. So, I would melt butter and pour it all over this healthy snack, giving it more calories than if I had popped it in oil to begin with! Nowadays you can even buy kettle corn, seasoned with sugar instead of salt.

A friend created a recipe that had neither sugar nor salt. Instead, he used just about every spice in his kitchen, from garlic powder to oregano and paprika, and called it Gourmet Popcorn. He passed away years ago and his recipe died with him. I wish I had written it down.

You could experiment. First, cook the popcorn in olive oil, coconut oil, or another type that is healthier than the usual non-specific vegetable or canola oil. Season the entire batch or offer various spices to your guests so they can create their own taste sensations. Include something with color, like paprika or cinnamon.

If you use white spices (garlic powder, onion salt, and parmesan cheese) you might over-season the popcorn without realizing it. And once it's seasoned, it's hard to get rid of the excess. You can't really wash it off.

Every once in a while, someone will mail me a single popcorn kernel that didn't pop. I'll get out a fresh kernel, tape it to a piece of paper and mail it back to them.
–Orville Redenbacher

5. Allow yourself one dessert a week.

I love eating chocolate cake and ice cream after a show. I almost justify it in my mind as, 'You were a good boy onstage and you did your show, so now you can have some cake and ice cream.'
–Steven Wright

If you're like me, you hate being deprived. This started when I was a girl and Mom told me I couldn't have a cookie. Instead of just accepting what she said, I obsessed over the cookie. That was all I thought about, so when I finally got one, I gobbled it down and asked for more.

Things haven't changed much. If I'm on a restrictive diet where I'm not allowed to eat sweets, there always seems to be a dessert calling my name, whether from the kitchen at home or from the menu or glass counter at a restaurant.

The only way I can get past all these unwanted signals is to allow myself one dessert. I might have one a day, but I try for only one a week. There are days when I can pass on the sugars and fats, but I find myself in the kitchen at 9 o'clock at night, looking for something to graze on. It's much better (and results in fewer calories) if I eat a small portion and satisfy the craving.

I went to a book launch at a friend's house where one of the treats was a s'mores station. She had mini-marshmallows, chocolate chips, and Teddy Grahams®, those tiny teddy-bear-shaped graham crackers. We put a mini-marshmallow on a toothpick and toasted it over a tea light candle, then made a miniature s'more. Yum! It's a tiny version of the super-sweet campfire treat and can satisfy my sweet tooth without breaking my diet. So on my way home, I bought all the ingredients.

If you're going to a party where there will be many desserts, try to eat a salad or an apple before you go to curb your appetite. A little trick that I learned many years ago was to eat dill pickle slices when I craved sweets. There's something about the dill that placates my sweet tooth.

Also, drinking a large glass of water before a meal can fill your stomach and keep you from eating so much. It's worth a try.

6. Enjoy dark chocolate—it's actually good for you!

All you need is love. But a little chocolate now and then doesn't hurt.
–Charles M. Schulz

We can finally eat chocolate without guilt.[23] It contains antioxidants and creates endorphins, those feel-good hormones we work so hard to get.

Darker chocolate has fewer calories and less fat than white or milk chocolate, so it's better for you. Bittersweet chocolate is great in chocolate chip cookies, but may not be great as a snack by itself. As the name implies, it's bitter. Lighter chocolates are semi-sweet, milk chocolate, and white chocolate.

Some people argue that white chocolate is a misnomer, since it doesn't really contain any cocoa. Candy coatings are usually made of white chocolate so they can be tinted and flavored. These are the worst for you, so limit your intake.

Of course, eating chocolate must be done in moderation, just like everything else. That's where snack-size candies come in handy. It's much easier to eat a bite-size candy bar or a Hershey's® kiss than to break a piece off a large bar and underestimate how many calories you're consuming. Not to mention fighting the urge to eat another piece … and another … Having them individually wrapped makes it easy to limit your treat.

Just because chocolate is good for you doesn't mean we can eat anything made with it. A piece of chocolate candy might be good; a piece of chocolate cake, not so good. Take into account everything else that's in the recipe, like sugar, flour, and oil. Those additional ingredients add more calories, making the desserts less healthy.

7. Give yourself a treat once in a while.

Nothing would be more tiresome than eating and drinking if God had not made them a pleasure as well as a necessity.
–Voltaire

All work and no play makes Jack a dull boy. Well, it's not just about work or Jack. If all you do is work hard and eat food that's good for you, you'll become not only bored but boring in the process. You need balance in all areas of your life.

When you're on a restrictive diet, you probably tell yourself that you can't eat certain foods. That's not bad, but it encourages you to focus on what you can't have. And we all know the result of that.

Instead of plugging away to lose "some" weight, create a goal to work toward. It doesn't have to be food-related, although it could be. If you tell yourself that you can't have dessert when you go to lunch with the girls, it's easier to stick to that if you remember that you'll have a treat later.

You could reward yourself by reading a good book for an hour or watching a movie on TV without folding laundry at the same time. Maybe you'd like a manicure, at home or in a shop. That's a luxury for me—giving myself time to let the polish dry and not getting up to do a chore.

If you're a workaholic like I am, you feel guilty just sitting, not doing something constructive. During my second marriage, my husband once told my grown son Brian, "Your mom and I sat on the couch last night and watched a movie together."

Brian responded, "Wait a minute. You mean my mother didn't get up every 10 minutes to go do something? She's never done that in her life."

My new husband had finally convinced me that laundry and dirty dishes could wait for a couple of hours while I took time for myself and him.

Find something that is a treat for you and reward yourself for something good you've done today. It could be that you stuck with your diet or exercised 30 minutes or kept your cool when that guy cut you off in traffic. As long as you have a treat waiting for you, it's easier to handle some of life's little annoyances.

8. Write down everything you eat.

My New Year's Resolution List usually starts with the desire to lose between ten and three thousand pounds.

–Nia Vardalos

Many folks pop things into their mouths without thinking. I think it's a throw-back from our toddler years when we did that with everything we picked up. The problem is that we can consume extra calories without even being aware we're doing it.

I have a seriously overweight friend who can't understand why she carries extra pounds when she eats normal-size portions at meals. Then I spent an afternoon at her house and watched her reach into the candy bowl many times and go to the kitchen for several snacks before dinner. Maybe she wasn't eating much at meals, but the in-between calories were literally killing her.

I need to keep track of everything I put into my mouth or I don't realize how much I've eaten. I write down everything I have for breakfast, lunch, dinner, and snack, then how many calories in each item. When I add them up, I know how much I've actually consumed.

If I have a snack, I write it in the book immediately and then total each meal and snack. When I realize how many calories I've consumed for the day, it stops me from eating more. I can also see how many calories I have left for dinner without going over my daily allotment.

Having 100-calorie snacks around helps, too. That way, I can have small treats so I don't feel deprived. When they're written in the book, I'm well aware of my eating habits.

Okay, confession time again. I don't always write down what I eat. That's when the scale starts sliding up and my size grows. It's especially hard when I'm travelling and have to eat out a lot. I tend to underestimate calories in restaurant or banquet food, and eat more than I thought. That's when I need to get back to my notebook and be more honest about how much I've gobbled down.

9. Drink lots of water.

Drinking water is like washing out your insides. The water will cleanse the system, fill you up, decrease your caloric load and improve the function of all your tissues.

–Kevin R. Stone

Most of us don't drink enough water to keep our kidneys and other organs functioning at optimum levels. According to the National Institutes of Health[24], when we're born, our bodies are 75% water. Later, we're only 55% water. That's why wrinkles appear—our skin dries out. We need to replenish what we've lost so we don't look like the California Raisins.

Many doctors recommend drinking 32 to 64 ounces of water a day.[25] That's one-half to a full gallon. Some say you should drink half your body weight in ounces.[26] So if you weigh 150 pounds, you should consume 75 ounces of water. Not sure I can do that, but I'm trying.

A friend has chronic kidney and bladder problems and can't figure out why. She uses a 6-ounce cup for her water and fills it three or four times in a day—not nearly enough to keep things working right.

When I drink water out of a glass, I sip and can take forever to finish it. But if I use a straw, I gulp much more water without noticing it. You've may have heard that using a straw increases wrinkles around your mouth.[27] That's true if you drink thick milkshakes every day. But drinking water through a straw has very little effect on your mouth muscles and the benefits outweigh any side effects.

Some folks don't like the taste of water alone. You could add a slice of lemon, lime or cucumber to your glass. It can make you feel less hungry and possibly speed up your metabolism. Mint leaves give a refreshing taste. Just don't get carried away with what you add to the water. You don't want it to be a smoothie instead.

Cranberry and blueberry juice are also good for you, but not as a replacement for H_2O. Consider them fruits, and limit them to one or two servings a day.

One other note—coffee, tea, and soft drinks do not count as water. Think of it as washing your insides like you wash your clothes. You wouldn't dream of using any of those other liquids to rinse laundry because your clothes wouldn't be clean.

Same goes with your body. Drinking plain water is best.

10. Get to and stay at a healthy weight.

Strength is the capacity to break a chocolate bar into four pieces with your bare hands—and then eat just one of the pieces.

–Judith Viorst

Not everyone is meant to be a size four, including me.

After hearing about health issues that excess weight can cause later in life, I wanted to drop a few pounds. I asked my husband if he felt I should go on a diet. Bryan's response was, "This is the size you were when I met you and when we married, so I like you the way you are. If you really want to lose weight, it's okay as long as you don't lose anything in your boobs or your butt." Well, when I lose weight, those are the first to go, so I tried another tactic.

I asked my doctor if I should diet for health reasons. He responded, "Your body is functioning well. Your blood pressure and cholesterol are under control. You're in good health, so I don't see the need for you to lose weight." That did it. I stayed where I was.

After Bryan died, I tried a fad diet and dropped three dress sizes. I looked fabulous and everything I wore in my new size fit without tugging or stretching.

The problem was, I didn't like restrictive eating, so I was happy only in the morning when I looked in the mirror. The rest of the day, I was miserable because I couldn't eat what I craved.

So I struck a happy medium: I ate the potatoes, bread, and chocolate that I loved, but only in moderation. Instead of a huge baked potato, I ate half and saved the rest for later. Believe it or not, a small cookie tastes just as good as a huge one. And it has far fewer calories.

Another thing I learned is that some men like a girl with curves. Had I been that teeny size when we met, Bryan wouldn't have given me a second look. But because I had some meat on my bones and clothes that looked great, he was interested and we had many happy years together.

A word of warning here: excess pounds can cause or aggravate chronic health problems,[28] such as pain in your lower body, especially your joints. If you ask a doctor, the first thing they'll say is to lose weight.

Many women, myself included, would balk at that and say that they can't lose anything and don't believe it would make a difference. But when I dropped just a few pounds, I was amazed at how much less my knees hurt. It can make a difference for you too.

11. Eat out seldom.

Honestly, I just go to restaurants to eat so I won't die.
–**Steven Wright**

We can get so busy that we spend less time sitting to eat meals. This is especially true of those who work outside the home but still have a family to feed. It's very tempting to stop for fast food, pick up something on the way home, or bundle everybody off to a restaurant for dinner.

Not only are those choices more expensive than cooking for ourselves, but they're usually less healthy. You can easily consume more calories without realizing it.

We tend to go to places that have really good food. But what makes it so good? Usually added butter or extra sugar. These are most noticed by taste buds on your tongue, so you decide from the first bite that you love it. As a result, you could put on extra weight just by sharing a meal with loved ones.

I'm not saying you should never eat out. Just try not to make it a daily practice. And if you do find yourself at a restaurant, here are a few ways make it healthier:

- Eat only half your hamburger's bun. Most burgers or sandwiches have one side of the bun with no condiments on it. Remove that half, then eat as usual. This trick alone can save you a hundred calories or more.

- Don't be tempted into super-sizing your meal. Most fast-food meals contain way more than you should eat at one sitting, so eating less can still satisfy you. I dump out all the fries and then eat only the ones cooked the way I like them—soft inside, crispy on the outside. When all that's left are the crunchy potato sticks, it's easy for me to leave them uneaten.

- Soda pop is loaded with calories, but diet sometimes has a funny taste. My friend Rosalee mixes one part regular pop with three parts diet. That way, three-fourths of her drink has no calories, which is a significant reduction. And she still gets the taste she loves. One combination she enjoys is Diet Pepsi with Mountain Dew. Come up with your own favorite, using more diet than sugared liquids.

- After you divide your meal so you only eat half, you don't need to take your leftovers home with you. Just leave the box on the table and you'll know you ate fewer calories. Of course, you could take the food and eat it the next day if you want, saving money as well.

12. Read labels.

There are three ingredients in the good life: learning, earning and yearning.

–Christopher Morley

Packaging can be attractive. Manufacturers purposely make their products appealing so we'll buy them. The problem comes when we buy something for its package, not for what's inside. Ingredients are usually listed in small type, making it hard for "old eyes" to read in poor grocery-store light. I think they plan that as well.

Whatever the problem with reading the label, we need to figure out how to do it. Ingredients are named in order of the amount per serving, with the largest component first. So if the list starts with sugar, there's more sugar than anything else inside; if egg is first, that's most prevalent. The federal government regulates this.

Another thing to be aware of is whether you can pronounce all the ingredients. There are times when I can't even begin to say "mono-unsolidificatinatalides" or whatever. (I made that up, so don't look for it anywhere but here.) If you can't say the word, chances are you don't know what it is and your body won't like it. You'll be much safer with more natural ingredients, like milk, flour, eggs, and fruit.

Beware of hidden ingredients in the list. Salt content may be an issue if you have a problem with high blood pressure. Hidden salt can create more problems than just weight gain and water retention. You may be counteracting your medications without realizing it.

When I went on a restrictive diet, we were advised to go through everything in the cupboard or pantry and remove anything with salt, also called sodium. I didn't think I had any in my kitchen. What a shock to find so many things, including seasonings, that had salt listed as an ingredient.

Substitutes like Mrs. Dash® are available. These contain other herbs and spices that trick your tongue into thinking it's getting salt while making your food tasty. It could take some getting used to, but you might find it quite refreshing. I like it!

One other surprising fact on labels is the amount and size of servings. I once bought an individual package of salted peanuts. It said a serving was 160 calories, so I allotted for that amount in my snack. Unfortunately, what I didn't notice was that the small bag contained 3.5 servings. That meant that if I ate that individual bag of peanuts, I would actually consume over 500 calories! I stopped before I emptied the bag, but not before I had eaten way more than I planned.

The number of servings in a soft drink can be misleading as well. Before you guzzle a can of soda pop, check how many calories you're consuming. A 12-ounce can might say that it has 140 calories per serving, but that little can contains one and a half or two servings. I guess they figure you add ice to fill a glass, so you could split the can between two people. However, you could drink 200 or more empty sugar calories without noticing.

Read everything on the label, not just the ingredients. If you think that would take too long, ask yourself: *Would I rather spend a few minutes reading what I'm putting in my body or 24 hours a day being unhealthy?*

The choice is yours.

The bottom line is simple: know what you're eating and drinking and how much. No one is forcing you to put things in your body, so take control.

So, when it comes to eating healthy, it's just doing the right thing. And it's not something you have to do 365 days a year, but I think it's something you have to do 25 days a month. Let's put it that way.
–Mike Ditka

Chapter 12

EXERCISE

I really believe the only way to stay healthy is to eat properly, get your rest, and exercise. If you don't exercise and do the other two, I still don't think it's going to help you that much.

–Mike Ditka

I have some friends who absolutely LOVE to exercise, sweat, and work out. Not me. I HATE to sweat and don't get a second wind when I run or ride a bike. In fact, I'm lucky to hold on to my first wind. So exercise is not and probably never will be one of my passions.

When I retired to write fulltime, I was living in a subdivision where few people were at home during the day. I felt uncomfortable walking around the block by myself and too self-conscious to go to the local recreation center. New home construction started in the neighborhood and there were all sorts of laborers around. Just not where I felt safe walking alone.

Watching television one day, I felt the urge to tap my foot to the music. Then, I got up and started marching in place. Before I knew it, I was walking back and forth in front of my coffee table, arms swinging and lungs expanding.

That became my exercise of choice. I can spend 20-30 minutes early in the day, power walking, kicking, chain-stepping, maybe even walking around the coffee table and then back the other way. It's not exactly a running track, but it gets me moving.

Maybe you feel the same about exercise as I do, but adding movement to your day is really easy. And it's something only you can do. Here are a few tips.

1. Use it or lose it.

It's challenging, but you have to at least try to eat right and exercise.
–Joely Fisher

I know, I know. You've heard this a thousand times and you're tired of it. But I'm here to tell you it's true. I found out firsthand that if you don't use your muscles, you lose them.

My husband Bryan was in a serious car accident and broke his left arm and right leg. He spent the next few months with daily exercises and weekly visits to the Physical Therapist to monitor his improvement. The PT told Bryan that she had done all she could to help his arm, but he should keep doing theS exercises.

The only thing Bryan remembered about that conversation was that she had done all she could. To him, that meant that he was totally healed. He quit doing his exercises and never fully regained the use of his hand.

When I was diagnosed with arthritis in my hands, I thought my days of playing piano were over. I would wake up with stiff joints and just want to soak them in hot water and whine about the pain. However, when I started opening and closing my hands every morning as my doctor recommended, my knuckles responded and began to move with ease. Typing on my computer and playing piano, the very things that had been difficult to do, were the solutions to the problem. The more I type or play now, the less pain I have.

The same is true of other muscles. If you've ever known someone who had a broken arm, you might have seen what that arm looked like when they removed the cast. The muscles atrophied, meaning they had become weaker and shrunk in size. The person then had to exercise even more to make the muscles strong again.

It's so much easier to stay in shape than to get in shape. I heard a rather plump friend say one time, "I AM in shape. Round is a shape!" We laughed, but that rhetoric didn't help her body function as well as it could. She had to work harder to streamline her body.

2. Exercise 20 minutes most days.

> *Exercise to stimulate, not to annihilate. The world wasn't formed in a day, and neither were we. Set small goals and build upon them.*
> **–Lee Haney**

Some folks like to spend an hour in a gym every day. They have lots of workout gear and carry a gym bag in their cars. But it's not absolutely necessary to work out for an hour at a stretch, as long as you get regular exercise. The key is to keep your body—your "machine"—oiled through regular use.

Unfortunately, life intervenes and you can't always find time for a workout. That's okay, as long as you exercise most days. When I know I'm going to a Colorado Rockies baseball game and walk a mile from where I park, I won't take my early morning walk at home. If I'll be loading and unloading my car with 30-pound boxes of books, I might pass on weight lifting that day. But I still move and use those muscles.

My knees don't fit together right and it hurts to go up or down stairs. So I have an elliptical in my bedroom to ride while watching the morning news. When I first got the machine, my knees could only take four minutes, then they were screaming at me and I was on painkillers the rest of the day. But I was determined, so I put on knee braces and kept at it, increasing a minute every few days.

I worked up to twenty-five minutes on the elliptical, but sometimes my knees tell me to stop sooner. I just listen to the aches and pains to find the right amount. The good news is that I've increased the amount of exercise I get.

Sometimes I just don't feel like exercising because I'm tired, depressed, or sick. That's when my body needs rest to get over whatever it's dealing with physically or emotionally. It's fine if you have the same problems. Just try not to avoid exercising all week long. You're just kidding yourself if you don't keep your body in shape.

God set the standard of rest on Sunday when he took six days to create the world and rested on the seventh. So give yourself a day off each week. Our bodies need rest, and if we don't allow time for that, we're harming them, not helping, and can't recover from overusing the muscles.

It's easier to maintain a routine if you exercise at the same time every day. I like mornings before I shower, in case I sweat. One friend goes to an exercise club mid-morning, after she's had breakfast with her husband. Some folks prefer the evening. Get your body used to moving at the same time every day and it will cooperate.

3. Vary your workout so you won't get bored.

Variety is important when it comes to exercise. I don't do anything that bores me to tears.

●   **–Alanis Morissette**

There was a time in my life when I was doing step exercises every day. I didn't have a little platform like you see on exercise videos, so I just used the stairs in my house. That limited how I moved, since I could only go up or down, not to either side.

The idea of step exercises is good, but it got old. Plus, it hurt. I was born with knee bones that didn't fit together correctly, so I was doing more harm than good. The pain made me lose interest and eventually I quit doing those exercises and started getting flabby again.

I switched to an elliptical, but after a few months, that got boring as well. When I alternated with other exercises, I discovered that variety made it more fun and easier to get in the mood for a workout. Now I decide what I feel like doing each morning. That way, I'm not in a rut and will likely exercise every day.

You might have the option of going to a gym or a spa that has equipment to work different parts of your body. There's one franchise that has all the exercise equipment in a circle, and you work your way around along with other ladies, accompanied by upbeat music. You spend about a minute on each contraption, and then shift to a space between where you just keep moving, and then on to the next gizmo.

When I visited, one lady barely moved as she worked her way around. She would get on a machine and do the minimum to make it move. Then, on the mat in between, she merely shuffled her feet. I doubt her heart rate increased at all. If she had given it some effort and done enough to breathe hard and maybe break a sweat, she might have noticed an improvement. And maybe she would have whittled down her pot belly.

A good way to see if you're getting enough exercise is to work at it enough to breathe hard and maybe perspire. I know, I know, you probably don't like to sweat. But your body does, and sometimes we have to do what we don't want to so that our bodies work more efficiently.

4. Reward yourself after exercising, but not with food.

> *I think exercise tests us in so many ways: our skills, our hearts, our ability to bounce back after setbacks. This is the inner beauty of sports and competition, and it can serve us all well as adult athletes.*
> **–Peggy Fleming**

Rewards are good. As a child, we were cheered when we took our first steps, applauded when we sang, "I'm a little teacup…" and rewarded when we tinkled in the potty. We've been conditioned to expect a prize after we succeed at anything.

I need to set a timer or keep track on a clock to be sure to get in all the movement I need. Otherwise, I get tired or bored and stop when I start breathing hard. That doesn't do my body any good.

My reward for completing all the minutes of exercise is that I get to play Sudoku on my laptop. That's normally a waste of time for me, but if I allow myself to play after exercising, it justifies the game. It's also exercising my brain logic muscles, so it's good for me too.

Find something you like to do that costs you nothing. Maybe it's sitting down to watch a movie, listening to a CD while reading a book by the fireplace, or giving yourself a facial with cucumbers and a mask. Whatever it is, save it for after you've completed your exercise for the day or for the week.

My friend Evelyn rewarded herself by putting a little money in a savings account. Then, when she had lost weight, she had funds to buy smaller clothes. It turned into a Win-Win situation.

5. Move while doing other activities.

Some of the best ideas I get seem to happen when I'm doing mindless manual labor or exercise. I'm not sure how that happens, but it leaves me free for remarkable ideas to occur.
–Chuck Palahniuk

We tend to get into a rut, doing the same things in the same way, from washing dishes to laundry to dusting. But a small change can make a big difference.

The easiest way to add movement is this: don't lie down when you can sit, sit when you can stand, stand when you can walk, or walk when you can run. Running burns more calories than walking, which burns more than standing, and so on. So stepping up a notch can increase your metabolism.

I first discovered this when I was blow-drying my hair. I always bend at the waist to dry my hair upside down so it will have more body and lift. One day, I was staring at my ankles and wondering why I was just standing there hanging my head.

I started moving—put my feet shoulder-width apart and did some lunges while I was drying the hair on the top of my head. When I started drying the right side, I switched to bounce-stretches, like I was attempting to touch my feet. Then, when I dried the left side, I put my feet together and continued bouncing. Just that little bit of movement got me started on the road to exercise.

One day I stood up from the couch and found myself dizzy and falling over to the side. The only other person ever I saw do that was my husband's 80-year-old grandfather losing his balance. He caught himself, but it alerted me to the fact that older people lose muscle tone in their body cores, which is why they tend to fall and can be seriously hurt. These are the muscles in the abdomen that maintain balance. That's when I decided to exercise my middle.

Now, when I'm doing my lunges and bending, I suck in my tummy muscles to the count of five while I dry the top of my head. (Squeeze-2-3-4-5-squeeze-7-8-9-10…) It takes six counts of five, or a total count of 30, for my hair to dry. Then ten counts of three while I dry the right side (Squeeze-2-3-squeeze-5-6…) and thirty individual counts for the left. That little bit has helped my balance and tightened my waist. A strong muscle core can also help ease back pain.[29]

Another way to add movement is to dance through your day. When vacuuming, bounce along with the machine. Brushing teeth, sorting laundry or frying ground beef are great times to do a little step-touch. Mow your own lawn and shovel your driveway. Take those outside-maintenance opportunities to do some deep breathing and keep your lungs working for many years to come.

6. Add a little walking to your errands.

The older I get, the less jarring I want my exercise to be.
I find that a long walk is equally as helpful
and satisfying as a three-mile jog.
–Kim Cattrall

My grandmother started walking three miles a day when she was sixty. Now she's eighty-seven and we have no idea where she is! That's a joke, so don't hang any MISSING posters.

Do you remember when indoor malls were first built? Everyone was thrilled to have all the stores under one roof. You could park your car and walk inside from one shop to another, going back to your car if you had drop off some purchases. Plus, malls were a great place for exercise buffs to do their walking in bad weather.

Now, malls are being torn down and we're back to stores with parking right outside the door. Instead of getting exercise by walking through a mall, we drive around until someone empties a close-in parking space. Then, after one purchase, we drive to the next shop and take ten steps inside.

When you go shopping, whether to a grocery or department store, drive past empty parking spaces near the door and tell yourself, "I'm not that old yet. I'll leave those for someone who can't walk very far. I'm in better shape than that." And park in a far-away space. That will add a few more steps each way.

Another thing to remember is that slow movement generally builds muscle[30]; faster movement can streamline and reduce fat. So if you want to bulk up your legs, add weights to your ankles and walk slowly. But if you want to reduce them in size and increase your metabolism, walk faster. It can increase your heart rate and breathing, which gives you more oxygen, gets your blood pumping, and improves how your body works and looks.

7. Suck in your stomach at red lights.

I have flabby thighs, but fortunately my stomach covers them.
–Joan Rivers

Okay, this one sounds a little weird. What does sucking in your stomach have to do with red lights? Well, I've already mentioned that we need to exercise our core muscles so we can maintain balance and avoid falling over. That means your stomach muscles need to be toned. Not only will you reduce the risk of falling, but imagine how you'll look when you tone an inch or two off the middle. It's another Win-Win.

Whenever you think of it during your day, suck in your tummy muscles and hold them for a while. You can maintain this a few seconds at a time and repeat it a lot or you can just hold tight for half a minute or so.

This where stopping for a red light comes in handy. Most red lights last a couple minutes, giving you an opportunity to focus on your tummy. And a red light can be a reminder.

After I shared this tip with friends, one of them thought it was such a good idea that she explained it to anyone riding in her car. Then, when they came to a red light, she announced, "Okay, everybody suck in your tummy muscles!" After 20 seconds or so, she said, "Relax. Now do it again." And they all got a mini-workout.

When you find yourself on the road a lot, maybe for work, vacation, or a road trip, squeeze your tummy whenever you think of it. My friend Patricia suggested that we squeeze our butt muscles as well while waiting for a traffic light. That's just a little toning you can do without much effort.

If you don't spend a lot of time in the car, you may need a different trigger to remind you. I work at home and usually have the television on for company. When the show goes to commercial, it's time for me to do my tummy "work-in."

After all, a little is better than none.

8. Make exercise a social event.

Find fitness with fun dancing. It is fun and makes you forget about the dreaded exercise.

–Paula Abdul

Everything is better with a friend, and that is especially true of exercise. There may be days when you just don't feel like getting in your 20 minutes. You'll do anything but put on those exercise clothes and work up a sweat.

That's when a friend can hold you accountable. When they show up at your door or call to remind you, it's hard to say no. A truly good friend will not let you say no, and they'll exercise right along with you, encouraging you to keep going.

It works in reverse, too. Your friend may need someone to get them moving. You could be the nudge they need.

This applies whether you go for a run/walk through the neighborhood or to a gym. Sign up for a class and get matching workout clothes. The more you're tied to each other, the more likely you are to stick to it.

My friend Rosalee goes to a ladies' workout every weekday morning. The place is open six days a week so she can go whenever she feels like it. Since she has no one to go with her, she has made friends with the manager, who expects her at a certain time every day. Rosalee doesn't want to disappoint her, so she shows up on a regular basis.

When you go for a walk, don't do like my mother-in-law and take one step … then another … and call it walking. That's just "extended standing." Instead, walk at a brisk pace to get your heart pumping and your breathing deeper. You could pretend John Phillip Sousa is directing the band and you're marching in a parade. Or take along some music and walk at the same tempo.

Here's another time a friend can help. When you get to a fast enough pace, you can no longer talk. Make a pact with your friend that you'll set a routine of several five to ten-minute segments: warm up, walk normally, pick up the pace, slow down, and cool down. You may even want to add more faster/slower segments in the middle.

Keep track of your progress. If you know your starting weight, Body Mass Index, resting heart rate, and measurements, you can see your improvement. Warning—if one of you is competitive, you may not want to share your stats with your friend. You don't want someone getting angry if she's not toning up as fast as you are.

I have enjoyed seeing and feeling the results of daily movement. My pants fit looser and I'm not out of breath as often. Plus, I can climb up and down stairs easier and play on the floor with my grandkids. Some friends are excited that they can cut their own toenails without a huge stomach in the way.

One other thing: if you weigh yourself regularly, don't get upset if you don't see any loss but your clothes fit better. Muscle weighs more than fat. So as you strengthen your muscles, your body will reduce in size but may stay the same weight. It's just repositioning and toning, but overall you'll be in better shape, physically and emotionally.

The number on your scale doesn't matter. What does matter is how you look and feel, and that you're taking control of your health. With enough exercise, you could be fabulous for years to come.

Anyone's life truly lived consists of work, sunshine, exercise, soap, plenty of fresh air, and a happy, contented spirit.
–Lily Langtry

Section 5

BEHAVIOR

Human behavior flows from three main sources: desire, emotion, and knowledge.

–Plato

No matter how good you look or what a great entrance you make at a party, if you behave poorly, you can destroy that façade. You could be a drop-dead-gorgeous runway model, but if you chomp a wad of gum, act rudely or crudely, or are totally ignorant of what's going on, that may be what you're remembered for, not how wonderful you look.

Many years ago, I attended self-improvement classes at a modeling school. My instructor was incredibly beautiful and turned heads everywhere she went.

I was behind her one day when she and a friend left the school. A man stood watching her with his tongue dragging on the ground.

She turned to her friend, took a drag on a cigarette, and spouted some profanity. The man snickered and looked away.

That was the turning point for me. I realized that being fabulous is about so much more than just looking great. Remember, this book is "Free to *Be* Fabulous," not "Free to *Look* Fabulous."

In this section, we'll observe how to relate, sleep better, and improve our surroundings, resulting in feeling and acting better. Try these suggestions and you'll be surprised how much more confident you can feel.

Chapter 13

RELATIONSHIPS

Treasure your relationships, not your possessions.
–Anthony J. D'Angelo

hen Bryan and I married, he felt uncomfortable in a crowd. He preferred to come home after work, have dinner, and watch TV until bedtime. At church, he was content to be a pew-warmer, not talking to anyone. I don't think he realized that he was marrying a social butterfly who wasn't happy sitting still.

I convinced Bryan to join me at functions with church groups and friends. At first he would sit by himself and sulk. But eventually he learned to ask questions and create small talk. He developed friendships and even looked forward to attending some get-togethers.

You and I were made to be in relationships. After God created the very first human, he said, "It is not good for the man to be alone. I will make a helper suitable for him." (Genesis 2:18) Note that he calls Eve a "helper" for Adam, not a slave. This isn't an editorial comment, just a fact.

It's still not good for anyone to be alone. You may be old enough to have heard Greta Garbo's famous line from the movie "Grand Hotel." She plays a famous Russian ballerina who wants to end it all. After disappearing from a performance, she returns to her hotel to find several people looking for her. To get them to leave, she says, "I want to be alone." When pressed further, she repeats, "I just want to be alone." Many people felt that Garbo was saying that about her personal life as well.

There will always be those who truly don't want anyone around. They're content to be alone. Let them be. You can't force someone to be with people if they don't want to.

This chapter is for those of us who want better relationships.

Start conversations by asking leading questions, ones that can't be answered with Yes or No. Ask things like, "What do you think about…?" or "How do you…?" or "Tell me about…" People love to talk about themselves, and they'll consider you a wonderful conversationalist and maybe a good friend.

You can learn how to broaden your circle of friends, maybe cultivate some new, healthy relationships. You might be surprised at how easy it is.

1. Create and maintain relationships.

God gives us relatives; thank God, we can choose our friends.
–Addison Mizner

Our earliest relationships are with those we didn't choose to be close to—our families. As we discover how we fit with parents, siblings, and other relatives, we understand what works or doesn't work. This carries forward with other acquaintances at preschool, church, school, even the bank.

Speaking of the bank, don't let money determine who your friends are. When teaching my school-aged son Tim how to handle money, I gave him enough cash on Monday to buy lunch all week at school. Tuesday morning, he wanted more. When I asked what happened to four days of lunch money, he said it was gone. "Some guys wanted to be my friend, so I bought their lunches." Needless to say, those "friends" disappeared as fast as Tim's money did.

That still happens as adults. If we have a little more than others or maybe win the lottery, folks can come out of the woodwork with their hands open. It's tempting to buy food, entertainment, or other stuff to keep them close, but they'll leave as soon as their personal ATM stops working.

Find someone you're comfortable with at church, at work, or at a party. They needn't be good-looking or smart, and they definitely don't need to be of the opposite sex. In fact, for this section, let's stick with same-sex relationships. Girls, find a girlfriend; and guys, find a guy pal. Making friends with someone of the same sex is often easier and less complicated than the opposite.

A relationship can start with just a smile and "Hello." But for it to continue, you need to dedicate time and effort to help it grow.

First, encourage your friend to talk about herself. The more you listen, the better her opinion of your friendship. You may know someone like that—they ask questions to get you talking about yourself, then sit back and let you talk. It's flattering to think that someone is hanging on your every word, so you might just naturally like them. Before you know it, you've become friends. Try doing it for someone else.

The thing that works best for me in developing a friendship is to find something we have in common, then talk about that. My writers group is made up of women with families, homes, and lives, but all of them are writing books. That's our common interest, so after talking about that, we branched out to discuss our personal lives. We've become close friends and support each other with more than just critiquing. In fact, our group begins each weak having lunch together and catching up on what's happening.

When Bryan was restoring a 1965 Falcon Tudor wagon, he joined the Mile Hi Falcon Club, looking for parts for his old car, but found so much more. The group welcomes spouses, not just the guys, so I attended with him. We became friends with other members, many of whom came to Bryan's funeral and drove their Falcons in his honor. I still belong to that group, years later, because of relationships that have grown.

Look around at the friends you already have. How could you be closer? Call someone to meet for coffee or send an email to reconnect with someone far away. Take a step to bring them closer and you could create the friendships you want, need, and deserve.

2. To have a friend, be a friend.

> *If you go looking for a friend, you're going to find they're scarce.*
> *If you go out to be a friend, you'll find them everywhere.*
> **–Zig Ziglar**

We need friends for a number of reasons: to talk to, to accompany us to a movie, to have dinner with, or to cry with us.

Some folks feel they're just fine alone, they can do everything and don't need anyone else. The Book of Ecclesiastes explains why this isn't good: "Two are better than one, because they have a good return for their labor. If either of them falls down, one can help the other up. But pity anyone who falls and has no one to help them up." (Eccl. 4:9-10)

My friend Barbara is a wonderful lady, always willing to help anyone with a problem. She has delivered meals to folks with health issues, chauffeured others to doctor's appointments, and visited many who were house-bound. So when Barbara found herself facing surgery, recovery, and cancer treatments, friends were eager to help. She had created her support system long before she needed it and without realizing it.

Bryan and I experienced the same thing. He was in a serious car accident that put him in a wheelchair for 18 months. During that time, folks brought meals, lent that wheelchair and a walker, and cleaned our house for us, things we would have had to pay someone for.

Do you want that kind of friend? Be that kind of friend. If someone mentions a need, see what you can do to help. When they don't have time to go to the store, offer to pick up some groceries when you're going. You can give them the receipt to reimburse you, but they'll be glad you took one task off their list.

In my book, *Stepping Through Cancer: A Guide for the Journey*, I recommend that you offer specific help. When I was taking care of my husband, a friend called and said, "Let me know what I can do for you." I told him I needed someone to mow my lawn. His response was, "Well, I can't do that, but if you have anything else, let me know."

In contrast, another friend called and said, "I'm making a pot of stew and peanut butter cookies on Tuesday. How about if my husband and I bring them over and share supper with you that night?" It was easy to say, "Yes." She offered something specific, a yes-or-no question, and I was very grateful.

An important thing a friend does is listen. Don't judge. Don't argue. Don't defend. Just listen.

My son was a difficult teenager during my second marriage. When Bryan complained about Tim's hygiene or his messy room, I was quick to jump in and defend him. I thought I was explaining well until the day that Bryan exploded. "You never listen!"

"What do you mean?" I replied. "I am listening."

"No, you're not. I'm trying to talk and you keep interrupting. Just let me tell you what's bothering me."

When I finally let him vent without correcting his facts, Bryan felt that I really listened. It hurt to hear those complaints about my son and not jump in and explain, but it was important to give Bryan my undivided attention. After he calmed down, we discussed the problems and devised solutions. Until then, he felt I was being stubborn and refusing to let him talk.

That's when I learned that a true friend wants you to talk and even encourages it. They can share your joys, cry with your hurts, and take your side in an argument.

You may already have some relationships like that. If not, look around and see whose side you'd like to take, who you can relate to. They may be your next best friend. Test the waters and see how close you could become.

Friendships are two-way. Don't wait for someone to call. Initiate it. Even if they don't respond to your invitation, you'll be glad you reached out. And call someone else!

3. Find the one thing all your relationships have in common.

In a relationship you have to open yourself up.
–Neil LaBute

We have so many ways of relating to people—we work together, attend the same church, shop at the same store, or belong to the same clubs. Our associations may be business, religious, convenient, or fanatical.

But there's one thing every one of your relationships has in common: You!

Folks in your neighborhood or across the world have the honor of knowing you. They want and deserve to know the real you, not just a profile you've posted online or a plastic face you wear on Sunday to cover up the person inside.

Dorothy and I attended church together when our sons were in trouble with the law. Our hearts ached for our teenagers, so we'd cry together if we talked about them. Instead, we would plaster on a smile, share a hug, and compliment each other on the plastic faces we wore so no one would see our hurt. We never really became friends, because we kept that smokescreen.

Had I let Dorothy see the real me, we might have developed a friendship where we could lean on each other. There was so much to learn about court and jail that Dorothy could have taught me, but I didn't ask. Instead of maintaining a close friendship, we haven't spoken since she moved away.

Not to say that we should tell everyone our feelings. That would scare people away. But if we know someone going through something we've already dealt with, we can share with them and create a bond.

4. Cultivate close relationships.

A relationship requires a lot of work and commitment.
–Greta Scacchi

Social media is popular and powerful. When I started writing, I learned that I needed hundreds, maybe thousands of followers and "Likes." I started inviting friends of my friends and relatives to be my friend, just to get the numbers up.

You know what? They're not really friends. They're just an icon on a screen hiding a real human.

However, there are people behind some of those icons whom I know personally and can call true friends. Some attend my church while others are across the country, but they're still close friends.

How? We've connected personally, we've shared intimate facts of our lives, and we really know each other. When Lori in Alaska asks for prayer, she knows that I will pray. If Shirley in Idaho has health problems, she can depend on me to approach God and give her a call. Becky knows me so well that she spends the night in my guest room when traveling through Colorado.

That's how good friends act toward one another.

So how do you cultivate close friendships? Share yourself. Promise to do things. And follow through.

Jesus gave us the Great Commandment. It's not "Do unto others before they get the chance to do unto you." Good friends don't look out only for themselves. We look out for those around us. "Do unto others as you would have them do unto you" (Luke 6:31) puts a different spin on it.

If you were recovering from surgery, what would you like someone to do for you? What if you're going through a divorce? What about Valentine's Day when you're single? Well, do that for someone who needs it—Take a meal, send an encouraging card or note, bring flowers and candy. Whatever you came up with is probably what your friend needs right now. Go do it.

Reach out to someone who needs you. You may need them tomorrow.

5. Get out and around people.

I'm not a hermit, but I definitely stay in a lot more than I used to.
–Derek Jeter

A year after Bryan died, I retired from my office job to start writing and speaking fulltime. It's been wonderful, not having to get up at oh-dark-thirty, drive through bumper-to-bumper traffic and spend hours in a cubicle staring at a computer screen.

Instead, I can stay in my pajamas and spend hours staring at a computer screen.

After a few weeks of getting up, showering, and doing my hair and makeup with nowhere to go, I decided I didn't need to do all that if I was staying home. So the next day, I showered and put on sweats. No makeup, no hair done, but comfy. That day, my son called to ask if we could meet for lunch in a half hour. OOPS! Now I do hair and makeup every day, just in case I get a last-minute invite.

Unfortunately, when winter came, it was easier to stay inside and not clean off the car windows or slide on the road. That worked great until I realized that I hadn't seen another human in three days. I was a recluse. Or was it a hermit?

That's when I decided it wasn't good for me to be alone. When I get out of the house and talk with someone, even if only to say "Thank you" at the grocery store, my creative juices get going and I feel energized.

So now I plan at least one thing to get me out of the house every day. It may be a trip to the grocery or post office, but at least I'm around people. Plus, we all need 15 minutes of sunshine every day, so it's healthy too.

Even if you don't have a car or ready transportation, find another way to get around. One friend goes for a walk around her neighborhood every day and has struck up conversations and friendships with other women who stay home. Another friend calls someone every day for a long talk. Sometimes her friend will pick her up or come over for lunch and spend time together.

Be creative and you can find ways to interact with others. It'll be worth the effort.

6. Greet everyone with a smile and look them in the eye.

Smile, for everyone lacks self-confidence and more than any other one thing a smile reassures them.

–Andre Maurois

When I was working in the Marketing Department of a large corporation, I watched salespeople. Some would only glance at the customer and shift uneasily from foot to foot. Those customers were hesitant to do business.

So what's the trick? When you meet or greet someone, look them squarely in the eye, not to threaten but to assure them that you're a friend. Then give them a smile with your whole face, not just a plastered-on grin.

Picture the people you feel most comfortable with. What do they do when they first catch sight of you? Turn and look the other way? Of course not. A smile spreads to let you know they're happy to see you.

Looking them in the eye is easy if there's nothing negative between you. If you have an issue with someone, work it out. That's what relationships are about. We've all hurt others and been hurt by them. But we can get past it and restore relationships if we want. Then we can be sincere in our greeting.

Even my ex-husband and I can look each other in the eye now, since we've settled all the issues between us. It took a while, but we're friends now—not as close as we once were, but friends nonetheless.

You can do it. Maybe not with an ex but with a sister, a cousin, or a longtime friend. They're worth it, and so are you!

7. Choose how to respond.

> *In our response lies our growth and our freedom.*
> **–Viktor E. Frankl**

One of my dad's favorite things was blaming others for his reactions. "You make me so mad." "I did that because of you." "What I did is your fault, so I'm going to punish you."

People have been blaming others since God caught Adam and Eve in the garden. Eve blamed the serpent for tempting her and Adam blamed God for providing the woman who gave him the apple.

The truth is that no one *makes* you angry. Your response is up to you.

When you touch a hot stove, you've learned to pull your hand away immediately. If you chose to keep your hand there, you'd blister your fingers.

Anger can be a similar response. Someone has "burned your fingers," and instead of pulling away, you decide to hurt more and blame them. It makes no sense, but neither does an angry reaction.

If a child spills milk, yelling at them upsets both of you and does nothing for your relationship. Instead, you could say quietly, "That's okay. I spill every once in a while. No big deal." And offer to help them clean it up. The choice is yours.

Next time someone cuts ahead of you in traffic or in the checkout line, think about your reaction: Do you *really* want to yell, have a tantrum, and act like a spoiled child? Or would you rather just let it go and keep your blood pressure in check?

Imagine what would happen if you lit your fuse. Is that how you want people to think of you? Instead, think of letting the offense go. What would that look like? Probably much calmer.

For the next three weeks, whenever something upsets you, stop. Take a deep breath and think what you want to say and do.

Choose wisely. You'll live with the consequences.

8. Call an old friend just to say Hi.

Security in a relationship lies neither in looking back to what it was, nor forward to what it might be, but living in the present and accepting it as it is now.

–Anne Morrow Lindbergh

We've all seen movies where the mother of adult children complains, "You never call. You never write. I guess you just don't care." That feeling can spread into other relationships.

There are friends we've lost contact with that we would like to stay that way. But there are others we might want to reconnect with. On social media, it's easy to find friends or distant relatives. But do we?

People go to high-school or family reunions and reconnect with folks they haven't seen in years. They find things to talk about; so can you. My friend Allison reconnected with her high-school sweetheart at a reunion. They were both single and rekindled their romance.

I found my high-school sweetheart on Facebook. He's been married to the same lady for years, and she let me know in the past that she felt threatened by me. So I won't "friend" him, since I don't want to break up a marriage. That's one instance where it may not be good to reconnect with an old friend.

When you get that urge to reach out and you won't be interfering in a relationship, do it. You never know how much impact you can have on someone who needs to hear your voice. Call someone today.

9. Learn to be content, with or without a man.

It's nice to be with someone, but I don't think you need to be in a relationship to feel complete. That would be really sad.
–Kristin Davis

When my husband died, he predicted that I would remarry within two years and let me know he was okay with it. More than two years have passed and I'm still single. I would prefer to have someone special in my life, but it hasn't worked out that way.

A while back, I met a man who wanted to marry me. We enjoyed each other's company and spent a lot of time together. A lot. Together. He was ALWAYS at my house.

I misinterpreted that as love and thought we were meant for each other. That "Love is blind" adage was alive and well. I couldn't see red flags that kept popping up. Instead of asking God what he had in mind, I told God what I wanted and asked for his blessing.

After a nasty breakup, I was alone again. Of course, I miss having someone to sit and watch TV or go to dinner. But I have friends to do that. I'd rather be alone than be with the wrong person for the rest of my life.

My husband Bryan wasn't a baseball fan, so we didn't go to many Rockies games, although I wanted to. Since his death, I've attended games with friends and even have season tickets. I can now enjoy my passion without feeling guilty.

I still do my hair and makeup to look good, but it's for me now, not for a man. And I don't have to worry that someone else may not like the way my hair decided to fall or how my clothes fit today.

Smile at that beautiful princess in the mirror, that child of God, every morning and say out loud, "I am a beautiful, vibrant, capable woman and I'm proud to be me. I don't need a man to complete my life."

There are some who would disagree because they need a man. But for us strong women, if a man comes into our lives, it will be by choice, not out of desperation.

We are woman! Hear us roar! Or maybe we should say, "Hear us cheer for our favorite baseball team!"

What we women need to do, instead of worrying about what we don't have, is just love what we do have.
–Cameron Diaz

Chapter 14

SLEEP

It is a common practice that a problem difficult at night is resolved in the morning after the committee of sleep has worked on it.
–John Steinbeck

I used to get up at 4:30 am to send my husband off to work and start my day. That in itself wasn't terrible. What made it bad was not going to bed until midnight or later, and trying to function on much less sleep than I needed.

I used to brag that I could get by on only four hours. But to be honest, I wasn't as sharp as I could have been. My brain didn't get the downtime it needed to recharge, so my thinking was a little fuzzy. I didn't admit it at the time, but I can see that now.

Like most women, I felt there was too much to do to go to bed at a decent hour. There were always dishes to wash, clothes to fold, and floors to vacuum. And if I didn't do those chores, who would? Certainly not my husband or my sons.

Then one day I realized that the men in my house didn't care if all the housework was done, so why should I? At 10:00 every night, I'd get ready for bed, no matter what I was working on. That way, I'd get enough sleep to get things done and still give my body and brain the rest they needed.

Now that I'm a writer, my creative juices tend to flow in the evening. It's hard to stem the tide at night when the words are coming out, but there are days when I have to just close my laptop and go to bed. If I stop writing in the middle of a sentence or a paragraph, it's easy to pick up the next day. So as long as my brain shuts off, I can get enough rest.

Here are a few tricks to help you sleep long and restfully.

1. Get enough sleep every night.

I always try to sleep for at least eight hours a night and, of course, water, water, water!

–Jennifer Aniston

Many studies have been conducted on the number of hours of sleep a person needs.[31] The results varied from 6 to 10 hours, but most people felt best with 7-8 hours of sleep on a regular basis. It's different for each of us.

When going to an office job, I could get by with 5-6 hours of sleep. Maybe I just convinced myself, and my body got used to it, even on weekends. Now that I'm a full-time writer and speaker, I do much better with 7 hours. In fact, my body lets me know when I've shortchanged myself and I need to catch up. I get cranky and susceptible to all the colds and infections floating around.

Just as children's sleep needs vary with age, adult's needs may increase or decrease as we get older. My grandparents used to eat dinner at 5 every evening so they could go to bed early. They knew that their bodies needed more sleep, and they usually got 9 hours a night. That extra rest helped them live long, productive lives into their 80's and 90's. I hope to do the same.

One way to know the right amount of sleep is to let yourself wake up without an alarm clock. Try it one day when you don't need to go to work. Instead of staying up late just because it's Friday night, go to bed at your usual time and let your body wake up when it's rested.

When you can get up at the same time on Saturday as you do the rest of the week, that's probably the right amount of rest. If you sleep until noon, rethink bedtime. Your body is telling you something.

As teenagers, my sons would stay up as late as possible during the week and sleep in on the weekends. They obviously weren't getting enough rest, because it was a battle to get them out of bed for school. I resorted to using a squirt bottle: If they were still in bed after I called them twice, I stood at the door of the bedroom and counted to three. "Three" was accompanied by a stream of water directed at someone's head. They knew it was coming, so if they still refused to get out of bed, they chose the consequences.

Now that they're adults, they've learned to give their bodies enough rest. And since one of them now has young children, he *can't* sleep until noon. Ever.

2. Eat a little something shortly before you go to bed.

> *Think in the morning. Act in the noon. Eat in the evening. Sleep in the night.*
>
> **–William Blake**

Some diets tell you not to eat after a certain time each evening. Food consumed late at night can take up residence on hips and thighs.

I've gone to banquets and on cruises where dinner was scheduled late in the evening. The resulting heartburn kept me awake most of the night. In fact, when I watch a movie or TV show and someone has a date for dinner at 8:30, I shudder to think what that would do to me.

But if I eat at a normal time, there might be 12 or more hours before breakfast. My body can't handle it. That nasty hypoglycemia attacks me in the morning. I get ravenous and shaky and eat all of my day's calories at breakfast to compensate. But if I have a small snack of about 100 calories around 8 or 9 pm instead, my body can handle the long time between meals.[32]

You may not have a condition like mine but you still need energy on a regular basis.

Divide the word breakfast and you have "break" and "fast"—break the fast of not eating since dinner. If you can keep your metabolism on an even keel, your body will thank you and your stomach will not be growling while you're trying to nod off.

Contrary to a fast-food restaurant's ads, we don't need a "Fourth Meal" late at night. Trying to sleep while your body is busy digesting food is hard, not to mention the upset stomach from lying down immediately.

My in-laws enjoyed a small bowl of cereal every night. I prefer a glass of milk and maybe a graham cracker. Not a lot of calories, but the protein in the milk carries me through the night. And dunking the graham cracker makes me feel like a kid again!

3. Go to bed and get up on a schedule, even on weekends.

There was never a child so lovely but his mother was glad to get him to sleep.

–Ralph Waldo Emerson

Sometimes going to bed on a schedule is easier said than done, especially when you're a social butterfly. Weekend events keep you out later than normal, and some movies on TV go into the late hours. As a result, you feel like sleeping in to give your body enough rest.

Your body has an internal clock, thermostat, and regulator. They tell you when it's time to eat, sleep, put on a sweater, or do many things every day. My friend's mother did such a good job teaching her to go to sleep and waking her on a schedule that she still goes to bed and wakens at the same times every day, 50 years later.

If you have a job with regular hours, lunch is probably at the same time every day. Your body becomes hungry then, knowing what's coming. Doing the same for your sleep gives your body the rest it needs. Your health will thank you.

Let your body keep you on track When you get hungry, eat. When you get sleepy, lie down to rest. When you're cold, put on a sweater. When it's bedtime, give in to it.

4. Use ear plugs or white noise.

Laugh, and the world laughs with you. Snore, and you sleep alone.
–Anthony Burgess

Hawaii is a beautiful place to vacation. Many hotels are on a beach, with the ocean's waves lapping at the sand, day and night. Some people find that restful. Not me.

When Bryan and I went to Hawaii for our anniversary, I was frustrated. I'm such a light sleeper, the sound of the ocean kept me awake. Even with the windows closed and air conditioner on, I could still hear the waves. You'd think a regular rhythm would be conducive to sleep, but wave motion is not quite regular. There's just enough difference between breakers for a musician to notice. It kept me awake all night long.

After one night without sleep, I bought ear plugs. They drowned out all sounds, including waves, snoring, and hotel guests going to their rooms after the bar closed. In fact, they worked so well that I used them after we returned home to muffle noises when my husband slept with the bedroom window open.

Another way of masking sounds is to have ambient or white noise. There are machines that create the hum of radio static, running water, birds, or wind through the trees. I have one that turns off after an hour. That's long enough to fall asleep so I can spend the rest of the night without depending on a noise-maker.

You could try relocating for a while. Bryan told me I "slept soundly" often, so when I got noisy, he'd go to the living room and sleep on the couch. At first, I was offended. But he had done the same with his late wife, so I tried not to take it personally.

Find what works for you. If it's not quiet enough to sleep, block out the noise or go somewhere else. No reason to stay put, lose sleep, and be miserable.

5. Invest in blackout drapes.

For sleep, one needs endless depths of blackness to sink into.
–Anne Morrow Lindbergh

When we bought a brand-new house, window coverings were not included. We had blinds installed, but not drapes, so as soon as the sun was up, I was, too. The first windows to get drapes were in the bedroom.

Most draperies are made for appearance, not to keep out light. You have to look for ones marked as such. If the package says they're "lined," that only means that there is one more layer of fabric, usually thin white cotton or something similar.

Blackout drapes do just what their name implies—they black out the window so light doesn't come in and wake you with the sun or a streetlight. This is especially important if your sleep cycle starts late at night and you need to keep resting beyond the 5:07 AM wake-up call the sun gives.

Also, if you want to nap in the afternoon, they're a great help. Those curtains can help you rest in a darkened room and be opened to let the sun in when you want it.

A friend told me she had wonderful drapes that made her room midnight-dark. There was no problem sleeping—or oversleeping! Your brain needs morning light to indicate that it's time to move from rest to motion, so open the drapes when it's time to wake up.

You could use an alarm clock that gradually brightens the room. When you set the alarm for 6:30 in the morning, the light starts coming on about a half hour earlier. By the time it buzzes or turns on the radio, your brain has registered that the sun is coming up and it's time to rise and shine—in more ways than one.

> *Your body tells you what it needs, and if you sleep past your alarm on a Saturday morning, it's probably because you need the sleep.*
> **–Sophia Bush**

6. Do only relaxing activities at night.

> *I sing seriously to my mom on the phone. To put her to sleep, I have to sing "Maria" from "West Side Story." When I hear her snoring, I hang up.*
>
> **–Adam Sandler**

I used to work with folks who would exercise for an hour at a gym before going home. They'd eat dinner and have no problem going to sleep, or at least that's what they said.

Once, when I didn't get my morning workout in, I figured I could work up a sweat before dinner. My heart was pumping and my muscles quivering, just like they're supposed to. Unfortunately, it got me so revived that I couldn't sleep. I felt like I'd had two cups of coffee with dinner—I couldn't shut things down to rest.

For me, any evening exercise gets my body and my brain wound up. So instead, I keep evening activities low-key. If I go to a movie, I make sure it's not a thriller that gets my heart surging or my mind imagining weird creatures chasing me. Those are only for afternoons.

Instead, watch a relaxing show or movie at night, nothing with fights, aliens, or murder investigations. That way, your dreams will be pleasant, not the frightening stuff that nightmares are made of.

7. If you don't fall asleep in 30 minutes, get up.

If you can't sleep, then get up and do something
instead of lying there worrying.
It's the worry that gets you, not the lack of sleep.
–Dale Carnegie

When you have a routine before you go to bed, your body gets the message: *I know what comes next. When you do things in this order, it's time to shut down the brain and sleep. Gotcha.*

Sometimes, you might interrupt the routine or your brain gets the wrong message. That's when "brain noise" takes over and sleep eludes you, no matter how hard you try. I used to lie in bed for an hour or two, looking at the clock and calculating how many hours I had left before the alarm. The math kept my brain working, which in turn kept me awake.

Now, if I haven't fallen asleep in a half hour, I go to the living room, turn on a light, get a glass of milk or a cup of herbal tea, read a book, watch television or do some writing. When I start to feel drowsy, I turn off the light and go through a mini-routine before I hop into bed. Then, my brain usually gets the idea, and I can sleep.

If you share a bed with a light sleeper, you'll need to be a little quieter. The TV might be too loud, but you can still go to another room for a while. Grab a book or write a thank-you note, maybe an encouraging email to someone. Then, quietly creep back to bed.

This trick worked many times for me, even though Bryan was easily awakened. And it helped me get the rest I needed.

Sleep is one of the most important beauty and attitude products you can use. And it's also one of the cheapest. It doesn't cost a thing and the returns on that investment are phenomenal.

We are such stuff as dreams are made on; and our little life is rounded with a sleep.

–William Shakespeare

Chapter 15

SURROUNDINGS

Why should we think upon things that are lovely?
Because thinking determines life.
It is a common habit to blame life upon the environment.
Environment modifies life but does not govern life.
The soul is stronger than its surroundings.
–William James

I grew up in a house furnished in Early Clutter. We had more stuff than we knew what to do with, and it was out where everyone could see it. There were knick-knacks on the coffee table and end tables, doilies and pictures on the piano, and plants and statuary on the window sills. Walls were covered with pictures and other framed art. No planning, just stuff.

Mom collected salt-and-pepper shakers and had over 1500 sets, all displayed in our dining room. Dad built cases to hold them and kept expanding them as the collection grew. I remember a window in the dining room when we moved into the house, but by the time I moved out, it had disappeared behind floor-to-ceiling display cases.

Among the chores assigned to me as a teen was dusting, which included all those lovely salt-and-pepper shakers. Talk about tedious! That's when I decided that my house would have in view only what was necessary, if it was at all within my power.

Clutter can interfere with a positive attitude, spoiling all the progress you've made toward fabulous. You slow down to look for things, forget to pay bills on time, and find that clothes you planned on wearing are dirty. You then must backtrack, taking more time than you wanted.

But when you look fabulous and you and your body are functioning fabulously, you feel better and it spreads to other areas of your life.

Obviously, we can't control everything but there are some areas we can change. Let's look at ways to extend fabulous to our surroundings.

1. Create a feeling of self-confidence with neatness.

Your outlook upon life, your estimate of yourself, your estimate of your value are largely colored by your environment.

Your whole career will be modified, shaped, molded by your surroundings, by the character of the people with whom you come in contact every day.

–Orison Swett Marden

I don't have a housekeeper. Tried it and didn't like someone coming into my house and seeing how messy it was. Besides, they "put things away" and I couldn't find them for days. I'd rather live knowing where my stuff is.

Not that I was a messy person, but I had a husband and two sons whose priorities didn't include neatness. Most of my after-work time was spent picking up after them, which really cut into my fabulosity. I threatened them with tossing out anything left overnight and threw away several big bags before it had any effect.

Later, I discovered how much calmer my life could be if I just kept things tidy. I tried to teach my kids to put things away, but they didn't catch on until they had their own homes.

Now, when I'm done with something, I put it away until the it next time. Besides taking less time, it makes me feel calmer, knowing everything is where it belongs and will save me time when I need to find it.

2. Don't drive a litterbug.

I think it's always important to be vigilant of what you're doing and aware of your surroundings.

–Leona Lewis

I know this one is stepping on some toes, but it's important.

Have you ever had a friend pick you up to drive somewhere and had to move things on the seat before you got in? Or even worse, you had to brush crumbs off the seat and got jelly on your hand in the process? It happened to me and was embarrassing for the car's owner.

Your car is private property and you can do with it as you want, but when you invite someone in, it's better if you don't smudge their clothes. That may be enough to lose a friend or ruin a skirt, like it did for me. But it's easy to prevent both.

First, keep a litterbag or a plastic grocery bag in the front seat so you can reach it when needed for trash. When you go to a drive-through window and get a bag of food, use that bag for all your trash and take it with you when you get out of the car.

Then there's the back seat. It's easy to toss things back there so you don't have to see them or put them away. If you look around, you'll see a lot of back-seat or truck-bed litterbags.

I keep a blanket in my car, in case it gets cold. The blanket starts out on the seat, but eventually slides to the floor. When I know I'll have someone back there, I make sure the blanket is out of the way. It's just a common courtesy. However, I don't always remember. Just ask some of my friends who accepted my offer of a ride at the last minute.

Tomorrow when you get out of your car, take with you the trash and whatever you put in the car. It's easier to keep it clean than to spend time cleaning it up. And less embarrassing than having your trash lying around and fermenting in the sun.

3. Focus on preventive maintenance.

> *Some people have a hard time getting rid of stuff. If that's you, pray for God to give you the courage to get rid of things you don't really need or things He wants you to give away. This will help keep your surroundings organized and clutter-free.*
>
> **–Joyce Meyer**

Almost everything in our life needs upkeep: hair, body, car, appliances, clothing, even relationships. Unfortunately, we can't just set them up the way we want and expect them to stay that way. That would be like planting grass, never watering or mowing, and expecting it to look fabulous forever.

It's much easier to keep things in shape than to get them back in shape after you've ignored them. Dieting is a good example. Keeping off excess weight is easier than losing extra pounds once they're at home on your hips.

Here are a few things to do regularly to reduce fixing or cleaning up later:

- Use a clothes hamper for dirty clothes. It keeps them off the floor.
- Put dirty dishes in the dishwasher or the sink instead of leaving them wherever you use them.
- When you're done with something, put it away. It won't take any more time to do it now than later, and there will be a lot less clutter.
- If you notice a tear or a missing button on clothing, fix it before laundering. The washer or dryer may just make it worse.

You'll be much less embarrassed when someone stops by unannounced if things are somewhat tidy. And when cleaning house, the chores will be easier.

Ben Franklin was right: "An ounce of prevention is worth a pound of cure."

4. Make your house a home.

But if each man could have his own house, a large garden to cultivate and healthy surroundings—then, I thought, there will be for them a better opportunity of a happy family life.
–George Cadbury

How do you feel when you enter someone's house? Warm and welcomed? Awkward and out of place? Afraid you'll break or soil something? Better yet, what is your friends' first impression when they walk into your house?

Create a sense of friendliness just by having sufficient lighting in your rooms and adding personal touches to your surroundings.

Decide what colors you like. Whether bright, dark, or neutral colors, they show what's going on in your life and your mind. For a change, you could try different colors. When I'm feeling down, instead of reverting to my black clothes, I wear springy colors to lighten my mood. Do the same with color in your home.

Start with neutral walls: off-white, beige, or gray. Add your favorite colors as accents. If your furniture is already in your favorite shades, add neutral accessories. It'll make the room feel coordinated and complete.

For my great room, I chose a beige seating arrangement: couch, loveseat, and rocker. Then I added an area rug of burgundy, beige, and brown and completed the look with burgundy print drapes and solid burgundy throw pillows. It didn't take a lot of creativity, but it looks well-coordinated, and people love its hominess. And beige furniture will make it easy to change colors later if I want.

You may prefer blue or green, maybe even yellow or purple. Make your favorite color the accent, not the main color in the room. If you start with a bright purple couch, there's not much you can add to the room to keep it from looking like gaudy. And changing the décor would involve some major purchases.

Put something on the walls. You don't need to cover every inch, but have things hanging that make you feel good. Photos, paintings, or calligraphy are good choices. A word of warning, though—if you want to "make a statement" with nude art, keep it in a room not everyone will be in. When I used a friend's restroom, she had old-west nude photos of herself and her husband hanging for all to see. I felt so uncomfortable, I never went back to her house.

Have a few things lying around to make the house look lived-in, but don't get carried away. A few books, magazines, and remote controls in the coffee table are okay, but clutter or hoarding can be overwhelming. This is where preventive maintenance from the previous section comes in handy. The fewer things around, the less picking up you'll need to do later.

5. Redecorate, even a little.

All great change in America begins at the dinner table.
–Ronald Reagan

No matter how wonderful your house, you can get tired of it. Just think how you'd feel with your Christmas decorations up all year long. No matter how much you enjoy the holidays, it would get old and you'd want something different.

Make a small change to lift your spirits. Add throw pillows in different colors or swap out some pictures. Get new lampshades or an area rug. Even a colorful blanket tossed over the back of the couch can add pizzazz.

You don't need to redecorate often. But if you're feeling a little bored and have a few dollars to spend, go for it. Buying new can be a little restrictive, so consider thrift stores. Most of my pillows and wall hangings were purchased used and cost far less than in department stores. Or you could try making some accessories. Many websites have easy instructions.

Try putting away $20 from each paycheck so you can redecorate without affecting your personal budget. That way, you can save toward a goal and know how much you have available. If you plan ahead, you can spend without worry and give your creative side a little nudge.

6. Welcome friends into your home.

Any celebration meal to which guests are invited, be they family or friends, should be an occasion for generous hospitality.
–Julian Baggini

What good is it to create a welcoming home if you don't share it with someone? It's like cooking a 20-pound turkey for a huge Thanksgiving feast when you're eating alone.

When Bryan was around, our house would spring to life when he came home from work. Instead of being just a place to eat and sleep, it became a cocoon of love and comfort. When he died, those feelings were harder for me to find. Now, I invite friends or family whenever possible to share my home and hospitality. The house once again springs to life with loved ones.

You can do the same. Once a week, once a month, or whenever, invite friends over. Make it a big affair or just a time to share snacks and watch a movie or sports event.

Don't feel like you have to do everything. People love to help, whether it's bringing their favorite snacks for a movie or a side dish for dinner. Give them the opportunity and take some pressure off yourself.

We used to visit my aunt and uncle for Thanksgiving dinner, where my aunt insisted on doing all the cooking and not letting anyone else bring food. Instead of being a family sharing the meal, we felt like guests being presented a feast. Not that I wanted any glory for my pumpkin pie, but I would have enjoyed the meal more if it included something I contributed.

When you extend an invitation, tell your guests that everyone is bringing something to share and let them decide what they want to donate. Someone may have a marvelous recipe for a dish they want to make, so give them that opportunity. If they don't offer, let them come and have fun. You can fill in the menu after you find out what everyone else is bringing.

Holiday or not, make it a special occasion. Use a beautiful tablecloth, good china, your grandmother's silver, and candles. We all have nice things we're saving for "someday" but there's no guarantee that someday will come. Use those special things today.

Fabulous surroundings can create fabulous feelings. By planning ahead and keeping your home comfortable, your attitude can improve. Try it. You'll like it!

It's important to determine which surroundings work best for you, and then build that environment to suit your needs.

–Marilu Henner

I don't believe you have to be better than everybody else.
I believe you have to be better than you ever thought you could be.
–Ken Venturi

So now you have the road map to Fabulous. There are many stops along this route, ways you can change yourself and your life, but only if you want.

Where you end up on the journey is totally up to you. You can take one step or all of them. Take time to enjoy the fabulous person you've become and never stop looking for ways to improve.

Your transformation can be like the metamorphosis of a butterfly.[33] It starts out as a tiny egg the size of a pin head. The egg hatches into a caterpillar and grows 100 times in size.

The next stage, the pupa, involves a chrysalis, where it looks like nothing is happening. But there are lots of changes going on inside, transforming into a beautiful individual, completely different from what it was to begin with.

That could be you, changing inside where no one can see, but becoming more beautiful than you ever imagined. Others may not see much difference at the beginning, but keep at it and they'll notice. Maybe it'll be a sparkle that wasn't in your eye before. Or a relaxed smile and improved attitude.

Of course it'll be a younger-looking you, because you're more aware and putting your best foot forward. But you'll be better than you ever thought possible.

> *You have brains in your head. You have feet in your shoes.*
> *You can steer yourself in any direction you choose.*
> *You're on your own, and you know what you know.*
> *And you are the guy [or girl] who'll decide where to go.*
> **—Dr. Seuss**[34]

About The Author

Debbie Hardy is fabulous. Her fabulous attitude shows in everything she says and does.

After all that Debbie has survived, from childhood abuse to divorce to widowhood and everything in between, she could be angry, bitter, and ugly to everyone around her. But she made a choice instead to be fabulous, which has kept her looking and acting much younger than others her age. And as a result she is now known as the Queen of Resilience.

Debbie's writing career began when her second husband was diagnosed with cancer. As an alternative to calling family and friends with updates, which Bryan would have overheard, she wrote emails.

Since Bryan's cancer was inoperable and untreatable, the news became worse. She asked God to show how she could share hope with her readers, not realizing that she had to have the hope first to share with others. She began putting encouragement into each message and discovered that she was a writer. Within months, her readership grew to over a thousand.

That was the turning point in Debbie's life. After Bryan's death, she retired from a corporate career to write fulltime. Since then, she has written *Stepping Through Cancer, A Guide for the Journey, a resource for cancer caregivers, and its accompanying handbook. She also wrote Steps in Writing and Publishing a Book for those who have a dream to get their books out.*

A Colorado resident, grandmother, and accomplished pianist, Debbie is a member of Advanced Writers and Speakers Association, National Speakers Association of Colorado, and several writers groups, where she mentors aspiring authors. She contributes to anthologies, writes devotions, and teaches at retreats, seminars, and writers' conferences.

Check out her website at www.DebbieHardy.com.

Endnotes

1   http://www.healthyblackwoman.com/do-dark-skinned-people-need-sun-screen/

2   Elisabeth Kubler-ross, *On Death and Dying: What the Dying Have to Teach Doctors, Nurses, Clergy, and Their Own Families,* (Scribner, 1997).

3   Ben Carson, M.D. and Cecil Murphey, *Gifted Hands: the Ben Carson Story* (Grand Rapids: Zondervan, 1990), 5.

4   http://www.brainyquote.com/quotes/quotes/e/elizabethe413823.html

5   http://www.brainyquote.com/quotes/quotes/j/joanlunden177601.html

6   http://en.wikipedia.org/wiki/Joan_Lunden

7   http://parade.com/55268/walterscott/joan-lunden-on-being-forced-out-of-good-morning-america-17-years-ago/

8 Taken from Charles R. Swindoll, *Day by Day with Charles Swindoll* (Nashville: W Publishing Group, 2000). Copyright © 2000 by Charles R. Swindoll, Inc.

9 "New Study Proves That Laughter Really Is The Best Medicine" by Yagana Shah, Huffington Post, 04/22/2014.

10 http://www.oprah.com/spirit/Know-When-to-Trust-Power-of-Silence

11 Lyrics by Mark Lee, from Third Day's album "Wire," released 5-4-2014, Provident Label Group, LLC

12 http://www.webmd.com/diet/features/eat-smart-healthier-brain

13 http://4mind4life.com/blog/2008/07/18/brain-foods-list-of-50-good-brain-foods/

14 http://healthland.time.com/2013/07/23/why-you-should-eat-breakfast-and-the-best-times-for-the-rest-of-the-days-meals/

15 http://www.smart-goals-guide.com/smart-goal.html

16 http://www.webmd.com/balance/features/give-your-body-boost-with-laughter

17 http://www.mayoclinic.org/healthy-living/adult-health/in-depth/dental/art-20047475

18 http://www.webmd.com/cholesterol-management/tc/high-cholesterol-overview

19 http://www.medicinenet.com/script/main/art.asp?articlekey=87059

20 http://www.nlm.nih.gov/medlineplus/ency/article/007196.htm

21 http://www.mayoclinic.org/healthy-living/weight-loss/expert-answers/slow-metabolism/faq-20058480

22 http://optimalbodyweight.com/qa/weight-loss-tips/body/starvation-mode-weight-loss

23 http://www.webmd.com/diet/news/20030827/dark-chocolate-is-healthy-chocolate

24 http://www.ncbi.nlm.nih.gov/pmc/articles/PMC2908954/

25 http://www.livestrong.com/article/463935-what-are-the-benefits-of-drinking-64-oz-of-water-every-day/

26 http://health.usnews.com/health-news/blogs/eat-run/2013/09/13/the-truth-about-how-much-water-you-should-really-drink

27 http://www.huffingtonpost.com/2012/08/28/straws-cause-lip-lines-wrinkles-beauty-myths_n_1834297.html

28 http://www.cdc.gov/obesity/adult/causes/index.html

29 http://www.webmd.com/back-pain/features/relieve-back-pain-with-core-strength-training

30 http://fitness.mercola.com/sites/fitness/archive/2012/05/11/benefits-of-super-slow-workouts.aspx

31 http://www.webmd.com/sleep-disorders/news/20101130/how-much-sleep-do-you-really-need

32 http://www.livestrong.com/article/320492-the-effects-of-eating-late-at-night/

33 http://www.thebutterflysite.com/life-cycle.shtml

34 Dr. Seuss, *Oh, the Places You'll Go!* (New York: Random House Children's Books, 1960).